THE
SECRET
OF NEXUS

THE
SECRET
OF NEXUS

Discover the hidden truth of leadership....

JEFF J. MILLER

AMBASSADOR INTERNATIONAL
GREENVILLE, SOUTH CAROLINA & BELFAST, NORTHERN IRELAND

www.ambassador-international.com

The Secret of Nexus

This is a fictional work. Names, characters, places and incidents either are the product of the author's imagination or are used fictitiously. Any resemblance to actual persons, living or dead, events or locations is entirely coincidental.

© 2012 by Jeff Miller

ISBN: 978-1-62020-113-8
eISBN: 978-1-62020-162-6

Cover Design and Typesetting: Matthew Mulder
E-book conversion: Anna Riebe

AMBASSADOR INTERNATIONAL
Emerald House
427 Wade Hampton Blvd.
Greenville, SC 29609, USA
www.ambassador-international.com

AMBASSADOR BOOKS
The Mount
2 Woodstock Link
Belfast, BT6 8DD, Northern Ireland, UK
www.ambassador-international.com

The colophon is a trademark of Ambassador

Dedication:

Kathy – I love being married to you. Thanks so much for supporting me during this project. You are the sweetest person I know and my best friend.

Karissa, Kelsey, & Reed – I love you three kids so much. I hope you realize how much I care for you. I feel blessed to have the opportunity to be your father.

Appreciation:

Dr. Samuel Lowry, you and your entire team at Ambassador International have been great to work with. Thanks so much for the guidance and direction.

Adam Blumer, your valuable input as an editor was so vital in completing this book. You are very gifted and I really enjoyed working with you.

"Leadership can bring many challenges and at times may feel overwhelming. Being a leader also offers many rewards as demonstrated in *The Secret of Nexus*. This story is captivating and the deep meaning behind it will inspire you to become more impactful in your own leadership roles."

—*Anne Beiler,*
Founder of Auntie Anne's Pretzels

"Jeff Miller weaves a compelling and inspiring modern-day parable. The leadership lessons will inform and the spiritual truths will encourage."

—*Blair Dowden,*
President of Huntington University

"This is an easy to read fictional story with a powerful message on how to manage your business that all leaders could benefit from. I was touched by the real message behind the story, and how that can affect our management principles"

—*Derald Bontrager,*
President & COO of Jayco RV Inc.

Contents

CHAPTER 1

Culture

As Garrett Thompson merged onto the North Carolina highway on his way to work that Monday morning, his mind drifted to his former career as a doctor. The female reporter on the other end of his cell call was doing an article about Nexus, Inc., and she wanted to talk to the top dog.

Top dog?

He shook his head. *Five years ago, I thought being a doctor was my calling. Amazing how much can change in only five years.*

"So tell me what happened," the reporter said. "A doctor one day. An entrepreneur the next. That doesn't happen to everybody."

He pictured himself on that exhausting day,

swimming laps in the hospital pool after his shift. "It's a simple story, really. After my workout, I reached for my usual sports drink and read the ingredients label for the first time. I was disappointed. Then I wondered if there were any healthier drinks on the market."

"And you didn't find much of anything, did you?"

"Nope. So I decided to design my own sports drink."

She chuckled. "And the rest, as they say, is history."

"Pretty much. Of course, I enjoyed being in the medical field for a while, but starting Nexus, Inc., has brought true meaning to my life."

"And I'd say you've done pretty well for yourself. Correct me if I'm wrong. According to the stats I found on the Internet, your company produces over fifteen million dollars' worth of health sports drinks and arthritis cream every year."

"That sounds about right."

"Amazing!"

"It still surprises me too."

After a few more questions, the reporter thanked him, said the story would appear in tomorrow's paper, and hung up.

As he neared Nexus, Garrett's thoughts shifted to his 9:00 a.m. management team meeting. He looked forward to seeing what his team would bring up for discussion today.

After getting settled in his office and checking his e-mail and voicemail, Garrett rose from his chair, planning to say good morning to his employees, as was his usual custom. But before he could, Marianne, his secretary, glided into his office, along with her customary cloud of exotic perfume. She lately had a spring in her step she hadn't before, and he knew why.

"Don't forget," she said. "You have a second secretary now, and she starts today."

"How could I possibly forget?" He grinned. "You haven't been able to talk about anything else for weeks."

"Well, she's just outside now, nice and early."

"Sounds like my kind of secretary."

"You said you wanted to give her a tour and introduce her around."

"And that's exactly what I intend to do." He could have delegated the tour to Marianne or someone else, but no. He wanted to give the new secretary the full Nexus family treatment and let her see that even the "top dog" wasn't too important to play host. "Why don't you call her in and introduce her?"

Her name was Julissa, and she didn't look a day over nineteen, with her slim build and shoulder-length blonde hair. Marianne said that in addition to being excellent with computers, Julissa was very detail oriented. Just what Nexus needed.

Julissa seemed nice enough, if a bit shy. On his way to the research and development lab, Garrett paused at a familiar office door and knocked. "This is the office of Erin Masden, who really has two roles here at Nexus."

"Two?" Julissa said.

"She's the controller and head of human resources. Erin is a brilliant numbers person and really excels in the accounting field."

Coming from the medical field, Garrett remembered, he'd had a lot to learn in the financial realm. That was why Erin was one of the first people he'd hired—and what would he have done without her?

"I've rarely met anyone as ambitious and straightforward as Erin," Garrett said. "Out of the six people on the leadership team, Erin helps keep the team together. You see, she has a way of moving beyond the boundaries of Controller and Human Resources so she can help in other areas of the business, but she does so in a way that's nonthreatening to others. Everyone knows she has the best interests of the business at heart, and everyone appreciates her support."

The door finally opened—Garrett suspected Erin had been taking an important call—and Erin stepped out to greet Julissa with a firm handshake.

Tall, slender, and in her mid-thirties, Erin waved Julissa into her office, and they chitchatted about Nexus while Julissa checked out Erin's crowded desk.

"I just love my job!" Erin shoved a reddish lock behind her ear. "In fact, I enjoy my career so much that my husband, Scott, and I decided that one child was enough." She gestured to the framed photo of a three-year-old girl with sparkling blue eyes and an impish grin.

"So what originally brought you to Nexus?" Julissa asked.

"I was initially attracted to it because I'm a huge health nut. Just ask Garrett here."

Garrett nodded. "Erin runs six miles a day."

"And I just love our healthy sports drinks." Erin leaned against the wall beside various framed photos showing races she'd run in and the medals she'd won. "But since I came, I've learned to love the culture Nexus promotes, and I really appreciate the value system Garrett endorses. We take pride in the quality of the products we produce.

And hey, you can't beat such an awesome family atmosphere in the work environment."

During the conversation lull, Garrett remembered Erin's weekend plans with her daughter. "So how was the zoo?"

Erin made a face. "They have some really strange-looking creatures there."

Always trying to lighten the mood, Garrett chuckled. "Sounds like some of the creatures around here."

Garrett knew she was busy and didn't want to intrude. He said good-bye and led Julissa over to the lab to see Kramer, the only biotechnologist on staff.

"Kramer Bristol heads up product development or research and development," Garrett said. "I've known him since before I left the medical field."

Julissa looked at him in surprise. "You were a doctor?"

He'd forgotten what she knew and didn't know. "Yeah, but actually my medical background has come in handy. Even though I don't have a PhD in biology like Kramer does, I have a good understanding of the science involved in making the drinks and creams Nexus produces."

"I heard that you made the first Nexus products in your basement. Is that just a rumor?"

"No, it's true. And that's why I have a real passion for what Kramer does."

Kramer didn't turn from his computer as they entered the lab and stood at his back. A confusing tangle of colored tables and boxes crowded his screen.

"This is Kramer." Garrett planted his hands on the researcher's shoulders. "He's one of the most laid-back individuals you'll ever meet."

Kramer swung his chair around, as if in surprise; they'd caught him chewing on the end of a pen, which he plunked down on his workstation. Black eyes, curly-black hair, and olive skin hinted at a Middle Eastern ancestry. Black-framed glasses with lenses thick enough to magnify his eyes perched on his thin nose.

"He's very courageous and honest," Garrett continued. "Two very good reasons why I appreciate him so much. Combine his honesty with the fact that he's very trustworthy, and now you know why he's such a valuable asset to Nexus."

Kramer grinned at Garrett, his cheeks pink. "Oh, please stop. You're embarrassing me."

"Morning, Kramer." Garrett chuckled. "Did you have a nice weekend?"

"Let's just say it was"—he hunted for the right

word—"uneventful. Which is always good."

Garrett introduced Julissa, and they shook hands.

Garrett said to Kramer, "After the management team this morning, I want to spend some time with you looking at the B228 project." He was aware of the excitement simmering in his voice. He glanced at Julissa. "You're probably wondering what B228 is."

She nodded.

"See, health drinks are what got Nexus started, but an arthritis cream Kramer and I developed revolutionized the industry. Nexus really went global after that."

"Now we're working hard on a project that could change everything," Kramer said

She arched an eyebrow, eyes drilling into Kramer. "Everything?"

Garrett nodded. "Everything in the medical field. But for now, the product is so top secret, I can't even tell you what it is. Once we finish our research, I'm sure you'll hear about it."

Kramer no doubt had work to do before the meeting, and Garrett didn't want to detain him. As they strode away, Garrett knew what *not* to say—that Kramer's success in his professional career had unfortunately failed to carry over into his personal life.

Julissa must have noticed the lack of photos on Kramer's desk.

"Does he have a family?" she asked.

"Two teenagers," Garrett replied.

There was no reason to share more of Kramer's personal life. Certainly not the fact that he had been divorced for eight years. The divorce had been the result of discovering that his wife was having an affair. That devastating experience was why he had such a hard time trusting anyone. He'd had a really tough time over the years, raising two children as a single father. For him, an uneventful weekend meant there had been no teen drama at his house.

Next they stopped by the production area, where John O'Hearn, the fiftyish production/warehouse manager with the bald head, sagging belly, and mischievous brown eyes, was busily collating spreadsheets—probably production data for this morning's meeting.

"Good morning, John," Garrett said. "Is everything running well out here?"

John gave him a thumbs-up, then headed down a hallway and out of sight.

Ah, yes. A man of few words. At least when his time is limited.

"Sorry. I guess you'll have to meet him later in the production meeting," Garrett said. "John's an interesting part of the Nexus 6."

"Nexus 6?" Julissa said. "What's that?"

"Oh, sorry. That's my six management team members who are mainly in charge of our products."

She nodded.

"John's a little bit old school, but he's very committed to the organization."

John was married and had three kids and five grandchildren. A real outdoorsman at heart, he enjoyed activities such as hiking and bird watching. An all-around nature fanatic, Garrett thought. John had a few negative traits. He could be overly judgmental, sometimes his short temper flared, and his questioning attitude often got under Garrett's skin. He also had trouble relating to the younger generation of workers—he thought they were spoiled, and nothing would persuade him otherwise.

As their way back to Garrett's office, they passed Derek Willard, who was busy at the copy machine. Garrett paused and patted Derek on the back. "Good morning, Derek. Ready for another big week?"

Derek looked up with a boyish grin and the flash of his hazel eyes. "Of course, boss. Every week needs to be like that, right?"

Garrett introduced Julissa. "Derek is head of the sales department, and his personality fits the job well—doesn't it, Derek?"

"If you say so." Derek ran thick fingers through his blond crew cut—either because he was nervous or because he had too much energy to stand still without fidgeting. Garrett knew the true reason was the latter.

"Do you know what I like best about you?" Garrett said. "You're bold, and you know how important it is to believe in what you're selling. That belief is one of the main reasons you joined the Nexus staff, isn't it?"

Derek gave Julissa the thumbs-up with both hands. "Absolutely. Our products are top-notch. I use them every day. But that's why I gotta run. Hey, talk to you at the meeting, Garrett." He headed toward his office in a half-sprint.

Garrett chuckled as they watched his retreat. "That's Derek. Always on the go." As they resumed walking, Garrett said, "As you might expect, his job requires him to be on the road a lot, but he doesn't mind."

Why would he mind? He was in his late twenties without a family of his own, and the job worked well for his lifestyle. Garrett was aware that Derek had very little contact with his parents. Julissa didn't need to know that Derek had come from an abusive background.

Garrett gave a self-deprecating shrug. "I guess we've worked together long enough that I've become a kind of father figure to him. He's a sharp kid, so it's all good." He glanced at his watch and saw that it was 8:50 a.m. "Well, I need to head to my office and see to a few things before the nine a.m. meeting. You probably want to get settled at your desk."

Julissa nodded. "I'm definitely eager to get started with work. Thank you for the opportunity."

He smiled at her. "You're very welcome. We're delighted to have you as part of our team. I'll see you in the meeting. You haven't seen everyone yet—I'm sure there'll be a few more introductions later."

At precisely 8:55 a.m., Julissa grabbed her steno pad and joined Garrett and Marianne on their way to the conference room. "I'll finish getting settled later," she said to them.

Garrett stepped into the conference room, expecting to be the first person there. Most of the staff pushed meeting deadlines a bit, but that just showed how busy they were. Today he was surprised to discover that the room wasn't vacant after all.

"Good morning, Carlton," Garrett said cheerfully. "How are you on this fine morning?"

"Great, Garrett. How are you?"

"Outstanding and looking forward to the new week."

Carlton Vance stood and stretched his slim, muscular frame. Startling blue eyes complemented a ruggedly handsome face. His black goatee looked like it could use a trim.

Garrett introduced Julissa, and Carlton accepted her handshake with a smile. Garrett expected that Julissa would be as smitten with Carlton as most of the women staff was.

"Carlton heads up our information services here at Nexus," Garrett said. "He's very talented and very good at what he does. Not bad for someone not yet thirty, huh, Carlton?"

Carlton grinned, clearly basking in Garrett's praise. With his model good looks, it was no wonder he dated a different girl every other week. At least, that's what the rumors said, but Garrett had little time for idle gossip.

Again, Garrett fell short of relating everything on his mind regarding Carlton, who certainly had his faults. For one, he assumed he was irreplaceable in his current role. That pride sometimes caused friction.

On the other hand, Carlton was eager to learn more about all aspects of the business, and Garrett appreciated that quality about him. While talk around the water cooler suggested that Carlton lived a bit on the wild side outside the office and might not be as trustworthy as he tried to appear, Garrett had chosen to give him the benefit of the doubt. Only recently had Carlton's decisions come to seem selfish and not always in the best interests of the team.

As Garrett turned on his iPad and waited for the rest of the team to arrive, he cast an appraising glance at Carlton, who was making small talk with Julissa. He couldn't shake the uneasy feeling he had come to experience lately when he was in Carlton's presence.

CHAPTER 2

Diversity

At precisely 9:00 a.m., Garrett took a quick look around the room. Kramer, John, Erin, Carlton, and Derek were present. Not to mention his secretaries. Everyone seemed to be on time except Kari, the head of Marketing and Customer Relations and the sixth member of the Nexus 6.

He rubbed his cleanly shaven jaw.

Hmm. This isn't the first time.

Though Kari was a loving person who was committed to her job, she had trouble balancing her three kids with her work schedule.

At 9:04 a.m., Garrett said, "Well, we can't wait any longer. Let's get started."

As with many of Garrett's Monday morning

management team meetings, they went around the room and shared highlights from their weekend. Other businessmen Garrett knew would find this practice to be a waste of time, but he strongly believed that the personal touch strengthened relationships and helped the team chemistry.

This may, in fact, be the most valuable time of the week.

"I'll go first," John volunteered. "My grandson, Brandon, may be the next Babe Ruth. He smacked two home runs this weekend, both in the same game."

"Who's Babe Ruth?" Kramer asked, adjusting his glasses.

After the roll of John's eyes, they went to the next person. After five minutes of sharing, they were ready to get down to business.

Kari flew into the room and squeezed her round frame into an empty seat, her cheeks reddening.

"So sorry," she said, eyes downcast.

Garrett gave her a quick nod. Her blue eyes betrayed her embarrassment. She knew she'd let him down.

Garrett began by going over the leading medical magazine's latest review of their arthritis cream. "Group, I want to make sure you realize that our products are not traditional in respect to the medical field. I guess a good word to use would be 'alternative.' So let's not get discouraged that this review is not as positive as we would like. We know based on sales that this is a good product."

He expected groans and eye rolls and wasn't disappointed. Nobody, himself included, enjoyed negative feedback after their hard work.

"There's no denying it," he said. "This kind of information makes it harder to sell our products. No doubt our distributors read our product reviews."

One by one team members chimed in, complaining about how unfair the review was. With some effort, Garrett refocused the meeting.

"We should be used to these types of reviews by now—we've worked through them before," he said. "Remember, our product results speak for themselves. We know our mission, and we'll continue to produce quality products for our customers. Let's not get too caught up in one or two reviews. It won't help us to be negative or feel sorry for ourselves."

Their facial expressions told him they knew he was right, but sometimes even he needed time to vent before becoming proactive. Perhaps that was why they respected his leadership; he always tried to be an optimistic person who led with purpose. Focusing on the greater mission was the right thing to do. Getting all bent out of shape over a review wasn't helpful.

Just when Garrett thought he had the group under control and negativity at bay, the room's vibe turned sour again when Carlton gave his IT department report and listed software upgrades he was working on. When he was done, Erin spoke up. It was impossible for Garrett to miss the tinge of desperation in her voice.

"Carlton, you've worked hard, and we all appreciate everything you've done, but I have a question."

Carlton raised his eyebrows—she had his attention. "Yes?"

"Will any of these upgrades help make our accounting software compatible with the software in our shipping and receiving departments?"

"It seems like we've discussed this in the past, haven't we?" Carlton stroked his goatee.

A few nods around the table.

Carlton met her gaze head on. "There's no current fix for that problem—I've tried to find one."

Erin shoved reddish bangs behind her ear. "I know you've tried, but—"

"Then why bring it up?" A mix of anger and

resentment heated his voice. "You already know I've done all I can."

Erin eased back into her chair and crossed her arms, eyes downcast. Tension rose in the room like smoke wafting from a snuffed-out candle.

Garrett bit his lip and decided not to intervene. Some problems resulted in a little conflict—it couldn't be helped—but maintaining mutual respect during these meetings was critical.

Carlton's tone had clearly crossed the line. Garrett wondered if others had sensed this as well.

Kari from marketing appeared to rise to Erin's de-fense—the women clearly playing offense today. "Erin makes a good point, but I wish compatibility was our only computer problem. The computers in our depart-ment are so slow that it takes ten minutes just to turn them on. Then they work so slow—we must lose at least a half hour of work every day."

Carlton scowled at Kari.

Before Garrett could mediate, John jumped into the fray. "Well, at least you have a computer, Kari. One of my guys has been waiting two weeks for a computer, so he just uses mine all the time."

Carlton slouched and glared at the tabletop. For all

Carlton's good looks, he could turn ugly in no time flat. Naturally, he was upset—he probably felt ganged up on. Garrett decided to smooth things over.

"Listen, the tech department is not as large as some of our other departments. We obviously have some issues to work out. Carlton had to be out of the office a couple days last week, but I'm sure he'll quickly get caught up. Right?"

He looked at Carlton, who nodded, though he was still sulking.

"Please have patience with the situations you're in," Garrett said. "Has everyone filled out the proper paperwork for the problems you just brought up?"

Everyone with a grievance nodded.

Garrett leaned back in his chair. Having multiple personalities could be a good or bad thing. Diversity could build a stronger team, but sometimes all the different personalities led to more conflict than he would have liked.

The last exchange between Carlton and the team had struck him as being disrespectful, but the computer problems *had* been frustrating. He'd been frustrated with the IT department too, but sometimes allowing other departments to openly share frustrations during a meeting was more effective than giving Carlton a speech about stepping things up. Garrett knew he had a tendency to try to control areas instead of letting problems work themselves out.

Last to report, John went over some of his normal production goals. Because he managed the largest staff, he usually reported on how they were doing. He had a good report until he reached the end, when he made a cynical jab about the lazy, self-centered Gen Y workers in his department.

John's remarks rankled Garrett, but he chose to reply gently. "John, maybe you just don't understand the younger workers."

John spread his hands. "What's there to understand?"

"I think they're very positive people to be around," Garrett said. "And they're really creative. Those are two qualities any boss should admire."

When John replied with a blank look, Garrett continued. "I realize they can be a little high maintenance sometimes. But it's your job to find the positives they offer and bring those out."

The Nexus 6 members were silent, their gazes bouncing back and forth between the two men. It was no mystery that everyone, including Garrett, wondered what John would say next.

He didn't disappoint.

"Did you know that one of my staff showed up the other day wearing flip-flops? Yes, flip-flops. This is a production facility!" John's indignant look eased into a smile.

Everyone, including Garrett, got a laugh out of John's old-school attitude.

"Okay, you've got a point," Garrett conceded. "But will you promise me you'll look for their positive qualities and not just their negative ones?"

John hung his head sheepishly. "Yes, boss."

Garrett headed to his office, concerned about the meeting's negativity. Kari's tardiness also bothered him, and he debated whether to say something to her. He didn't want to overreact, but her poor behavior had become a habit.

Should be an interesting week.

He headed over to the research and development lab to spend a few minutes with Kramer before lunch. Though he'd spent countless hours in this lab with Kramer, the conversation always refreshed him and helped him stay focused on the mission.

Garrett took a seat across from Kramer's desk. "How's that B228 project coming along?"

"I'm close." Kramer pushed his glasses up to the bridge of his nose. "I feel like we've made some great progress in the last month, but I'm still missing something. Would you mind looking through those two reports and seeing if anything jumps out at you?"

"I'd be glad to. You know, I've got a report for you too . . . straight from Erin's desk."

Kramer grimaced; he shared Garrett's frustration. They'd needed to spend a lot of money on this area of the project, but they couldn't turn back now.

Kramer accepted the statement and glanced through the expenses to ensure they were correct. Then, for a full minute, they studied copies of the same report in silence.

Garrett tried to lighten the mood. "Kramer, you know this process needs to produce more electrons, right?"

Kramer said with sarcasm, "Really? Is that what you get paid the big bucks to say?"

They both chuckled.

Garrett could tell that Kramer had made a lot of progress. "It looks like you've been able to slow down the oxidation process in the body. That's great. I hope you know how grateful I am for your hard work and dedication."

Kramer smiled. "Thanks, Garrett."

"Kramer, the report you're looking at from Erin says we're severely over budget on this project. What can we do to curtail expenses?"

"I have some ideas. Do you mind if I keep this report overnight and get you some answers by tomorrow afternoon?"

"Sure. I might do the same with your reports, if that's okay."

"That's fine, but Garrett, this information is sensitive and—"

"Stop. I know this can't be seen by anyone. I invented that speech, and now you're giving it back to me?" Garrett smirked.

Kramer put his hands up. "All right, boss. That's enough. Let's go get some lunch."

Garrett arrived at the lab door first and pulled it open. Then, he stepped back in surprise. Carlton stood just on the other side. It was almost as if he'd been there all along, listening and waiting.

"Do you need one of us?" Garrett said quizzically. "We're just headed to lunch."

Carlton shook his head and stepped back as Garrett and Kramer stepped into the hall. "It's nothing that can't wait until after lunch. Do you guys mind if I tag along?"

"No, that would be great."

Garrett kept his voice upbeat, but all the while his mind was working. Had Carlton been listening in on their conversation? If so, why? Had they said anything they wouldn't want others to know? Carlton was always ready to learn more about the company, but some things simply couldn't be shared yet. Garrett filed the questions away for later.

CHAPTER 3

Accountability

At two, Garrett strolled to Marianne's desk. "In case anyone calls or tries to find me, I'm heading to the production area to visit John."

"Thanks for letting me know." Marianne turned to Julissa, who sat beside her and appeared to be undergoing some training. "Garrett likes to meet with John every two weeks, if not every week."

"I'll be back later," Garrett said. "So long."

As he headed down the corridor, Garrett reviewed some of the things he planned to say and knew that John might not like it. He needed to revisit the negativity John had displayed in the meeting that morning. Now was as good a time as any to address some issues that had been festering under the surface for some time. Would

John take his comments in the right spirit?

John greeted Garrett, and they met for a half hour, going over normal operations that included production output numbers, inventory figures, and employee overtime from the last two weeks. Next, Garrett brought up the computer situation in John's area, since John had shared the problem in the meeting.

"John, you know the two of us meet together at least every two weeks. But even though we try to stay connected, I had no idea your department was lacking the computers you need to work efficiently."

John backpedaled. "Though we do need to see improvements, the problem may have sounded a little worse this morning than it really is. I do have a request on Carlton's desk for the machine I need."

Relief washed over Garrett that the situation was not as bad as John had made it sound, but he was still disappointed that John hadn't mentioned his frustration before the meeting with the whole management team.

"John, you've worked with me for some time now. Do you have any idea how I would have preferred you to handle this situation?"

John gave Garrett a sheepish look. "Yeah, you would have wanted me to communicate the problem directly to you earlier. I shouldn't have let the situation get me so irritated that I displayed negativity in the meeting. Sorry, Garrett. I know your door is always open to me."

"No problem. John. You know me pretty well by now, right?"

"Sure."

Garrett smiled. "Then what issue do you think I want to address next?"

John rubbed his hand across his bald head as he pondered Garrett's question. "I'm afraid I don't know."

"I'd like to discuss your attitude toward some of your employees."

Defensiveness crept into John's brown eyes. "Garrett, you don't understand some of these people. They're just so lazy." He shook his head. "I have no patience for that."

Garrett nodded. "I understand your frustration—I have the same concerns. There *are* some employees who won't change and need to be terminated. But we also need to realize that not every employee can be managed the same way."

John looked puzzled; the lines in his forehead deepened. "Garrett, I treat everyone equally. I'm not into special treatment of anyone on my staff."

"That's not what I mean. I believe holding everyone to the same standard is important, but how you motivate and communicate with employees can't be the same for every person. They're all unique."

The concept seemed foreign to John. "Can you explain more?"

"Sure. You need to learn how to manage some of your employees differently than others. For example, Generation Y'ers grew up multitasking, so you need to think of ways they can do more than one thing at once. They also want to have a relationship with you so they're comfortable working through situations with you. And"—he hesitated—"you could learn how to text. They prefer that over traditional phone calls."

John thought for a moment and sighed. Suddenly, his demeanor seemed to change. "Garrett, it's true I've had some problems relating to my employees. I need to work on that. For some time, I've had problems relating to my own child too. I'm worried about Sam, my youngest. He seems to be searching for something, but I'm afraid he's searching in the wrong places."

Garrett tilted his head. "What do you mean?"

"Well, he's turned his back on our family and hangs out with a bad crowd. Garrett, I'm not sure what that will mean for him, but I'm a little worried. This conversation about relating to employees makes me think that maybe I didn't apply myself to understand him when he was younger. That could have contributed to where he is in his life."

Garrett paused to consider John's words. "John, you know you're a good father and grandfather. I would be careful not to blame this on yourself. You know, if there's anything I can do to help you or your family, just say the word. I'll be glad to help."

Garrett said this knowing that he needed to keep a healthy employee/employer relationship with John. But he also cared about John's family and wanted to lend his support.

Later, Garrett met with Carlton to go over their normal agenda as well as the IT issues that had come up in the meeting. He pushed aside his doubts about Carlton and tried to keep an open mind.

"Carlton, I'm wondering if we need a more formal way to keep track of projects and deadlines."

Carlton pressed his palms together and nodded. "I've had some difficulty meeting deadlines. A more organized system is probably what I need."

They brainstormed for a few minutes to develop a

spreadsheet that would show outstanding requests, dates of inception, goal of completion time, current status, and other important items.

"I wonder if this spreadsheet is something you could update before our weekly meetings," Garrett suggested. "Then we could go over it on a more consistent basis."

Carlton combed his fingers through his wavy black hair. "It's something simple I probably should have created a long time ago. I also think it'll help my assistant stay on task better too." He picked up his pen. "You know, we'll update this every afternoon."

The conversation encouraged Garrett. If he could access the spreadsheet daily, he could keep track of how projects were going and let other employees know the status when they asked.

Carlton's attitude also encouraged him. Was this the same guy who'd given him an uneasy feeling preceding this morning's meeting? Was this the same guy who'd been waiting on the other side of the door as if eavesdropping on his conversation with Kramer?

Maybe I've been mistaken about him.

Garrett looked him in the eye. "Carlton, the great thing about your job is that you're always solving problems for people. The worst part about your job is that you're always dealing with problems."

Carlton tilted his head and glanced down at the report. "You know, I love my job—I really do—but . . ." He paused as if choosing his words carefully. "I would also love some exposure to other areas of the business some day."

"What do you mean?"

Carlton met Garrett's gaze. "For example, I'm really fascinated with the research and development area of our business. I don't have any experience in it, but I find it really interesting."

Research and development was one of Garrett's passions too, so he understood the interest. But he was unsure whether the department was a good fit for Carlton. He loved it when his employees wanted to learn more and expand their interest in the business, but the fact that Carlton wasn't keeping up in his own department concerned him.

How could I possibly move Carlton to R&D if he doesn't seem to be on top of things in IT?

Garrett took a deep breath. "I appreciate your interest in other areas—really I do. I'll think about what you said, but before I can consider it, I'd like to see your own department run in such a way that other team members feel like they're getting the proper service. Let's focus on that for a few months, okay?"

A spasm of disappointment flickered across Carlton's lean face. "I understand, Garrett. You're probably right."

Later, Garrett was finally getting some work done in his office when his smartphone chimed. Margret, his wife, had texted him to let him know dinner would be ready in twenty minutes. Dinner with his family was always one of his day's highlights, and it was already 6:00 p.m. But he'd hardly made a dent in everything that needed his oversight. He would try to arrive on time for dinner, but he would have to come to work early in the morning to get caught up.

He texted her back. "C U soon."

Five minutes later, Garrett cruised the streets of Monroe, North Carolina, with his sunroof open and the windows down. He breathed in the fresh, warm summer air that swirled around his head.

The quaint town offered a downtown that thrived like towns had thirty years ago. Garrett drove by the park, where some kids played basketball on the center court.

If only I had more time . . .

He had a sudden mental snapshot—the smiling faces of his kids, Carter and Jasmine, when they'd played basketball there not long ago. He'd love to take them back. Maybe soon. And the park was so convenient, only a short walk from their house.

Garrett turned onto Shade Avenue, which was lined with big maples and oaks, and waved at his gray-haired neighbor—what was his name?—before turning onto his driveway and parking in his garage. Through the back door he entered the sunny kitchen, where Margret was putting the finishing touches on dinner: meatloaf with green peas and mashed potatoes.

He greeted her and gave her a peck on the cheek. Her long, brown hair was pulled back into a ponytail. The scent of something pretty lingered around her hair. She asked how his day had been.

"Fine. Nothing unusual to report."

"How's the new secretary?"

"Very sweet. She'll fit in just fine." He inhaled. "Dinner smells good!"

He stepped into the hallway and glanced to his left. Carter and Jasmine were doing their homework at the family room desk.

"Hey, Dad!" they called.

"Hey, kids. How was your day?"

"Fine."

"It was all right."

Guilt stabbed him when he recalled that morning's newspaper interview. What had he said? That Nexus gave true meaning to his life? He wished now that he had said things differently.

Nexus gave his life vision, but his family gave him true meaning.

My wife and my kids—those are the three most important people in my life.

Yes, that's what he wished he'd added. But it was too late now.

He returned to the kitchen and glanced through the mail that lay in a basket on the counter. Margret rushed to and fro, working so hard to present a wonderful dinner. He asked what he could do to help, and she put him to work.

While he set the table, he shook his head.

So much can change in two years.

Two years ago, he'd realized he was spending more time at Nexus than at home—and that his family was suffering as a result. That was when he'd made the concerted effort to strengthen his management team.

Because the team was stronger now, he carried fewer responsibilities and enjoyed a stronger home life.

Shortly after dinner, Garrett's smartphone rang. He glanced at the caller ID, and his chest tightened.

Jerry. The private investigator he'd hired six months ago.

He tried to breathe as he headed to the den and closed the door to take the call in privacy. Instantly, his palms were moist, his mouth Sahara dry. He stood at the window and peered out at the lush green lawn. "Hello, this is Garrett."

"Garrett, I'm glad I got a hold of you," Jerry said in his strong New York accent. "I've got some important news."

Not *wonderful* news. *Important* news.

Garrett leaned against the window frame for support and wished Margret was there to hold his hand. Strangely, now that the moment of revelation was here, part of him wanted to hear. Yet, part of him didn't.

He didn't want his life to change, and this could change everything. For good or ill.

What if it was bad news? Maybe he never should have called Jerry to begin with.

"I've located your father."

Garrett's legs weakened. He decided to sit down.

He's not dead after all. He's alive.

"Garrett, he lives in Detroit, Michigan. I've got all of his contact information right here, and I'm e-mailing it to you now."

Raw emotion pummeled him. Tears stung his eyes.

My Dad's in Detroit. He's been alive. All this time.

But what happened? Why did he give me up for adoption?

"Garrett, are you there?"

He remembered to swallow. "Yes, I'm here." Finally, almost afraid to ask, he said, "Any news on my mother?"

"No, but you could always ask your father."

Garrett closed his eyes. All energy had drained out of him. "Jerry, thanks so much for the information and for your hard work on this."

"You're welcome."

End call.

Garrett glanced at the home computer perched on the desk in the corner. Where Jerry's e-mail was waiting.

Your father's mailing address. Your father's phone number. Your father's e-mail address.

Your father.

Garrett raked a hand through his thinning black hair and stepped toward the computer.

He stopped. Blotted his sweaty hands on his pants.

Took a deep breath to steady himself.

No, not yet. He needed more time. Time to take all this in.

Part of him bristled.

Can you believe this? After all these years of wanting to know about your parents, you're too scared to open an e-mail?

Carter burst into the den. "Hey, Dad!"

Garrett whirled toward him, pulse quickening. How many times had he told Carter to knock first?

"Dad, can we go outside and shoot off my rocket now?"

Garrett struggled to compose himself. He wiped the moisture from his eyes.

The silver rocket lay in Carter's hand. How could he say no?

"Dad, are you all right?"

Garrett forced a smile. "Sure. I'm fine."

His son's eyebrows were raised. He probably realized he'd walked into something. Something Garrett wasn't ready to explain. At least, not yet.

Garrett worked to hide it. He smiled. "Let's go shoot off a rocket."

They headed outdoors.

CHAPTER 4

Teamwork

Garrett waited until after lunch on Tuesday before opening the e-mail from Jerry on his computer at Nexus. As he read about his father, a flood of competing emotions washed over him.

Of course, like many adopted children, he knew he wasn't unusual. He didn't need Margret to tell him that he'd struggled with feelings of rejection for years. The unanswered question of why his biological parents had given him away was one he'd grappled with for a long time.

He lifted his chin. *Too long.*

He stared at his father's name.

Tom Cooper.

My last name was Cooper.

He eyed his father's e-mail address.

A sudden barrage of new fears told him to wait.

Are you really ready to take that step?

He may not even reply to the e-mail. In fact, he could reject you all over again.

On Wednesday, Garrett was surprised when the editor of a national health magazine called and said he'd heard good buzz about the recent newspaper article about Nexus. He also wanted to do an article about Nexus, this one about the reasons behind Nexus's sudden growth.

How could Garrett say no?

"I'm very happy to hear that you'd like to do the article," Garrett said. But deep down, he wrestled with this opportunity.

True, he'd become a big part of the Monroe community over the last couple of years, involved with local service clubs, church, and even the library. Combine that with being president of Nexus and a former doctor in the region, and his profile in the community was high. Nonetheless, everyone knew he kept a down-to-earth perspective on life and didn't like bringing attention to himself.

An article for the local paper was one thing. This was a national magazine.

"Could you describe your goals for Nexus?" the reporter asked.

Garrett measured his words. "First, we want to produce quality drinks and creams to promote long-term good health. Second, we want our products to be affordable so the average person can use them. We want to help people be healthy. That's probably the biggest part of our mission."

The reporter asked a few more questions, then concluded with, "Why is the name of your company *Nexus*, and what does it mean?"

"*Nexus* is defined as a means of connection. I like the concept of connecting things, people, and product together. So we decided to name the company Nexus, Inc."

That concluded the interview.

Wednesday passed quickly. It was late Thursday afternoon when Garrett's phone rang. It was John from production. He wondered if Garrett had time to drop by and talk to him about a problem.

Uh-oh.

Garrett asked Marianne to reschedule his afternoon appointments and went to see John.

"What's up?" Garrett asked.

John's face was a mask of frustration. "The packaging machine broke down at about one this afternoon. By the time the maintenance guy got here, it was one thirty."

Garrett tried not to show his frustration at the half-hour delay. "What was he doing before he came to work on your machine?"

"I'm not sure, but once he did get here, it took him another two and a half hours to fix it!"

Garrett winced. "What were your employees doing during this time?"

"I kept them busy with other stuff, but now they're ready to go home. The problem is, we've got an order going out first thing in the morning, but we haven't started packaging it yet!"

Garrett shook his head. "Delaying the order is out of the question. We need to get the order packaged before we head home."

John nodded. "I agree with you. I'll tell everybody we need to stay three more hours and get the job done."

Garrett knew what John wanted to say but didn't. Nobody liked to stay late. And he could easily walk away and leave them to their jobs, but that wasn't his style. He'd helped on the line before, and John probably wondered if he would again.

"C'mon." Garrett started rolling up his sleeves and headed toward the packing line. "I'll help."

John grinned. "Now we're talking!"

John's staff smiled at Garrett as they worked side by side to get the job done.

Kari passed by production on her way out and paused with a startled look to see so many people still working. Then her eyes widened when she saw Garrett working on the line.

"Garrett, is there anything I can do to help?" she asked.

"Could you call my wife and tell her I won't be home for dinner?"

"No problem. Anything else?"

"Would you mind running to the pizza joint and getting four extra-large pizzas for the crew?"

She nodded with a grin and headed out.

Several other managers who were leaving for the day changed their plans and stayed to help too. As they worked and sweated together, Garrett couldn't help thinking how much he enjoyed his team of managers and employees. Sometimes managing people seemed really hard, but when they took ownership and assumed responsibility to accomplish something important, the result made it all worth it.

The pizza finished off the long evening, and everyone dug in.

"Thanks so much for your extra-hard work tonight," Garrett told the crew. "You went the extra mile, and I really appreciate it. Go ahead and come in a couple of hours later tomorrow. You've earned it!"

Everybody cheered.

On Friday morning, Derek was preparing to leave on a sales road trip later that day and dropped by Kari's office for their scheduled meeting at eight. She had marketing items he'd need for his presentations.

Her office window was dark. Obviously, nobody was home.

He glanced at his watch. 7:58 a.m.

Okay, I'll give her a break. It's not eight yet.

But at 8:05 a.m., he sighed and started pacing, frustration energizing his steps. By 8:10 a.m., he paced more quickly and clenched his fists.

Kari appeared at the end of the hallway and rushed toward her office door, key in hand. "I'm so sorry I'm late for our meeting. Were you waiting long?"

"I was here just before eight." He kept his voice steady and decided not to say what he was really feeling. But when she looked at his face, he was sure she could tell he wasn't happy she'd kept him waiting.

Kari rushed into her office, brushing kinky brown hair out of her face. She barely fit around the side of her desk to get to her chair. Derek looked away, wondering what someone with an obvious weight problem was doing working for a company that manufactured health products.

Kari faced him, out of breath. "Little Ben wasn't feeling very well this morning, so I had to find a babysitter for him."

Derek took a chair and mentally shrugged off her excuse. He just wanted the marketing materials.

They met for roughly fifteen minutes. With the materials he'd been waiting for in hand, Derek got up and turned to leave, then stopped. He decided to make one last impression.

"You know, all of us have deadlines to meet. Life's a lot tougher when you're late to everything."

Kari got up from her chair and stared at him as if she'd been struck. "Everything? I'm late to *everything*?" Anger smoldered in her eyes.

He tried to soften his words. "Well, maybe not to *everything*, but it does happen a lot."

Kari thrust her hands to her hips, voice shaking. "Maybe it hasn't occurred to you that I have a very good reason for being late."

"Kari, we all work hard, but there's no excuse—"

"You're single. What do you know about being a mom and looking after small children?"

"Well, I—"

"Absolutely nothing—that's what. Then, on top of all that, I work a full-time job because my family really needs the money. You know, I really don't appreciate—"

Erin knocked on Kari's door and peered into the room. "Um, is everything okay in here?"

Kari smoothed her hair back with a trembling hand. "Of course, everything's fine. I believe Derek was just leaving."

"Great," Erin said, opening the door wider. "Since you're leaving, Derek, do you mind stopping by my office for a minute?"

"Sure. Not a problem."

Uh-oh.

When he reached Erin's office, she gestured to a chair and took a seat at her desk. "So what's up? Is everything all right between you and Kari?"

He shrugged. "Sure. We're fine."

She met his gaze and held it. "I overheard part of your conversation, and it didn't sound very fine to me. You sounded like you were getting ready to draw swords."

Derek wondered whether he should just keep his mouth shut, but honesty overruled. "You know, it seems like a double standard."

"What do you mean?"

"Garrett always tells us that work is work and that we shouldn't let our personal lives interfere. But that doesn't seem to be true for everyone here, is it?"

Erin nodded. "Point taken."

"We had a meeting scheduled at eight. She could at least have called and told me she was running late."

"Let me work on the situation with Kari, okay?" She hesitated. "You also need to work on handling your frustrations in the right way."

He hung his head and regretted his remark to Kari.

"As you know, I head up the Human Resource department," she said. "Garrett is Kari's direct manager. I don't believe you've ever discussed this problem with us before."

Derek nodded. "Okay, Erin, I understand. You're right. I should have said something before it came to this."

After Derek left, Erin took a few minutes to collect

her thoughts, then headed over to Kari's office. She knocked on Kari's open door. Kari looked up with troubled eyes.

"Kari, are you okay?"

Her smile seemed fake. "Sure, I'm fine. I just don't understand why being ten minutes late is such a big deal."

Erin slipped into the chair across from Kari's desk and drew in a deep breath. Kari's tardiness wasn't a one-time incident and needed to be dealt with . . . but with gentleness. "Did you have a meeting scheduled with Derek?"

"Yeah. We were planning to meet at eight, but I had to take care of little Ben. He's not feeling so good." Her chin began to tremble, and her eyes moistened.

"Why didn't you call Derek and let him know you were running late?"

"I thought I could make it on time, but I got caught in traffic. You're right, I probably should have called."

Erin paused, giving her words careful thought before speaking. Juggling three kids with her work schedule couldn't be easy for Kari. Yet she was always optimistic and obviously loved being part of the Nexus 6, even though she faced numerous challenges. For one, she'd graduated from college twenty years ago with a marketing degree, but so much had changed since then. Customer expectations couldn't be easy to keep up with, and she knew Kari worked hard to stay in tune with what customers wanted. She'd even plunged into social media and taken Nexus to new heights in that arena.

If only she wasn't late so often . . .

Erin said, "You know that Garrett is a very understanding person to work for. He always gives us freedom to take care of things that come up in our lives. At the same time, he also has high standards for us, and everyone has the same standards to live up to. I've seen you use that freedom when you really didn't need to." She paused to let her words sink in.

Kari nodded slowly.

"Try to save your times of being late to work for when you really need to be late, like this morning. When you're late on a regular basis, you become characterized by that behavior. Then, when you really need to be late, your coworkers and managers have little patience for it."

Kari blinked a few times while processing Erin's words. "I don't know that I abuse the freedom Garrett gives us."

Erin rested her chin on her fist. "Why were you late to Monday's meeting? Honestly?"

Kari blushed and looked away. "Well, I really wanted to get some coffee before the meeting, and the line was longer than I thought it would be." She sighed. "Okay, you don't have to say anymore. I understand what you're implying."

Erin knew Kari had gotten the point. Before leaving her office, Erin encouraged her by listing the positive qualities she brought to the team. Later, Erin sent Garrett an e-mail, detailing her conversations with Derek and Kari that morning to keep him informed of the conflict and resolution.

On Friday night, after the kids were in bed, Garrett sat at his desk in the den with Margret. Together they crafted an e-mail to his father, Tom. They let him know who they were and asked him about possibly scheduling a phone conversation next week.

Garrett wiped the sweat off his forehead.

Margret put her arm around him. "Why are you so nervous about this?"

"If he doesn't respond, I'll feel rejected all over again."

She gave him a squeeze. "Well, we won't know until we try."

At 9:52 p.m., Garrett's hands were shaking when he clicked on "send." Every few minutes he refreshed his e-mail program to see if he would get an immediate response. But he didn't. By 11:00 p.m., Margret urged him to go to bed and get some rest.

When Garrett woke at 5:00 a.m., he couldn't help but run to his computer. There, sitting in his in-box, was a message from his father's e-mail address. He stared at the message, wanting to open it and not wanting to open it—all at the same time. Finally, he mustered his courage and clicked on the message:

Garrett, thanks so much for contacting me. I would love to have a phone conversation as soon as possible. I can't tell you how good it is to hear from you. I look forward to talking to you and getting in touch.

Garrett sighed with relief.

My father wants to talk to me!

Though he still had a knot of emotions to untangle, the fact that his father hadn't rejected him was a good start. But then when Garrett began to draft a reply, he realized something. He'd rather talk to his father face-to-face than talk on the phone.

He looked over his schedule for the coming week and noticed that Thursday was open. He drafted an e-mail suggesting a time and place to meet in Detroit on Thursday. By the time he sent the e-mail, floorboards creaked overhead. Margret was awake.

He ran up to their bedroom to tell her the news.

"He e-mailed me back. Can you believe it?"

"That's wonderful. What did he say?"

His voice shook while he told her.

"This is so exciting—I can't believe it!" She hugged him, then turned quiet for a moment. "Garrett, I wonder how your parents will feel about this. You haven't even told them about your search for your birth parents, have you?"

He shook his head.

"I think you should call them and let them know what's going on."

"You're right. I will."

They headed downstairs to the kitchen. For the next hour over breakfast, they talked about this wonderful development in Garrett's life.

Chapter 5

Reward

It was time for another Monday morning meeting at Nexus. When Garrett arrived at the conference room, he was pleased to see that Kari was already there, waiting for everyone else to arrive. They gave each other a polite nod.

Amazingly, everyone was in the room by 9:00 a.m. The team seemed to be in a good mood for a Monday morning meeting. Carlton told a rather exhausting story about his Saturday night date. Because everyone got a good laugh out of it, Garrett let him finish his story before starting the meeting at 9:03 a.m. He knew some of the staff were coming off an exhausting week and could use some encouragement.

He started the meeting in an unusual way. He asked

them to share something they appreciated about the person sitting to their left. Because he knew Erin would start things off right, he asked her to go first.

Derek looked at Erin expectantly and waited.

"Derek, you really care about your job," she said after a moment of thought. "You're diligent in your preparation for your sales calls. You do a good job of selling our products, and that is a benefit for all of us." She paused, deep in thought. "Your greatest gift is relating to your reps and potential vendors. They seem to trust you, and that trust extends to our products."

Derek stared at the table but smiled as if encouraged.

They kept going around the room until it was Carlton's turn to share. The person to Carlton's left happened to be Garrett.

Carlton cleared his throat and turned his blue eyes toward his boss. "Garrett, what I appreciate the most about you is your trust for your employees. I have worked for employers who didn't trust their employees. That can be disheartening. But I know it's different at Nexus."

Carlton's sentiment pleased Garrett. He placed a high value on trust. After thanking Carlton, he took a moment to share the good news about finding his biological father. Several stunned faces stared back at him. Not everyone had been aware that he was adopted. He announced that he'd be out of the office on Thursday.

After the entire group had finished sharing, the meeting moved on to reports. During their individual reports, Derek brought up his idea of starting a supplemental line to go along with Nexus's drinks and creams. Garrett had thought of doing this before, but he'd been hesitant. He could tell from the discussion, however, that some in the group were really excited about the idea. He had always encouraged his employees to think about the future and what products could make Nexus better.

Maybe it's time to take this step.

"So what do you think, Garrett?" Derek asked, leaning forward.

Garrett smiled. He'd remained silent for a reason.

Finally, he said, "I try to balance enthusiasm for 'thinking outside the box' with knowing there are risks when you diversify your products away from your core. It takes a lot of energy to start something new like that, and sometimes energy is lost from what you already do."

Several nodded.

He went on. "Nexus has grown a lot over the past five years. Sometimes I wonder if it has grown too fast. This doesn't mean I'm saying no, but I think we need to plan a separate meeting to discuss the idea of a supplemental line a little more."

After all the individual reports, Garrett went over a sobering report from the FDA. "Team, the report in my hand isn't good. We've been cited for a violation!"

Jaws dropped around the table.

"According to this documentation," he continued, "we've incorrectly labeled the ingredients in one of our drinks." He heard the disappointment and frustration ringing in his own voice, and their faces registered that they'd heard it too.

"Obviously, I don't need to tell you how important it is for our labels to be accurate," he said. "This violation was a minor one, but it could have been major."

Kramer, Kari, and John spoke up. Though they graciously agreed to work on the problem as soon as the meeting was over, Garrett knew that *he* was ultimately responsible to ensure they did not make mistakes like this.

"We're all a team," he said, "and this is just as much my responsibility as it is yours. But let's try really hard not to let this happen again." Garrett moved on to better news, based on the report in his hand. "Last month's sales were good—so good, in fact, that we broke a record for most sales ever in one month!"

The entire group cheered, and they were in a much better mood now. He knew they'd be even happier when they heard what he said next.

When they quieted, he said, "To celebrate this historic accomplishment and to show my gratitude for your hard work, I'm taking all of you out for lunch today!"

Another cheer.

* * *

When John returned to production after lunch, he checked on his guys in the receiving area. An employee he didn't initially recognize called him over and questioned one of the skids of product they were shipping out.

"John, this skid says we're not charging for the shipping or billing the customer for the product. Is that correct?"

John realized this employee was new—that's why he hadn't recognized him right away. "Yeah, Jack. Nexus ships out free skids of product to different charity organizations all the time. That's why you see 'donation product' stamped on the side."

Jack had a puzzled look on his face. "Why would we do that?"

John explained that many companies donated lots of money and goods to charitable organizations. "The reason Garrett has us do it is because he feels it's important to give some of Nexus's profits back to charitable organizations that need help. Trust me, it's a cool thing he does for others."

★ ★ ★

On Tuesday morning, Kramer strolled into the lab earlier than usual, hoping to get a head start on another busy day. He reached his work station and stopped.

Carlton's back was turned to Kramer. He was seated in Kramer's chair and doing something on his computer.

"What are you doing?" Kramer didn't regret the tone of accusation in his voice.

Carlton jumped up as if startled and spun around to face Kramer. "Oh . . . um, good morning. I . . . I was just . . . just doing some updates on your computer."

Kramer pushed up his glasses and eyed him suspiciously.

Carlton's blue eyes were wide, and he seemed short of breath. As if he'd been caught doing something wrong.

Just updates, huh? Then why act so rattled?

Kramer took a step closer. His eyes flicked from

Carlton to the computer, then back again.

Carlton pressed a hand to his chest and chuckled, as if trying to make light of the moment. "Wow, you really startled me."

Nice try. Perhaps he wasn't expecting me so early.

Kramer recalled the day he and Garrett had been discussing B228 in his office. They'd bumped into Carlton just outside the lab door, as if he'd been listening in on their conversation. If information about the product were to fall into the wrong hands . . .

Kramer leaned against the wall, arms folded across his chest. "I haven't seen you work on my computer before. Why are you doing it now?"

Carlton pulled at his goatee. "There are some really nasty viruses I've been tracking. The last thing you want is your computer to get infected. Your computer is so important around here."

"Why is my computer so important?"

Carlton blinked in surprise. "Well, isn't it obvious?" He gestured toward the screen. "Your computer contains all the information about our latest research. That seems pretty important to me."

Kramer kept a poker face because he knew something Carlton didn't—that he didn't keep the most secret information on his computer. He trusted no one at Nexus but Garrett. Some people had complained behind his back that he had a trust problem. So be it. When it came to the security of Nexus, he didn't think he could be too careful.

Kramer shrugged. "Okay, but you didn't answer my question. Why are you doing this now? I thought I had a policy with your department not to do any upgrades on my computer unless I'm present."

Sweat beads popped out on Carlton's upper lip. There was no mistaking that he was still on the hot seat. "Sorry, Kramer. I've tried to respect your wishes, but as you know, our department has too much on its plate as it is."

Kramer nodded. That was certainly true.

"The only way we can keep up is to do upgrades before everyone shows up for work. If you really want to be here during upgrades, sure, that's no problem . . . as long as you're willing to be here at five a.m."

"Five a.m.?"

Carlton nodded. "We can't very well do upgrades when everyone is working on their computers."

What Carlton said made sense.

But he should have told me he couldn't honor my policy.

Something inside told Kramer this wasn't the right

time to push the issue.

Just let him go. Don't make a fuss.

Kramer cleared his throat. "So are you about done?"

The relieved look on Carlton's face was unmistakable. "Yep. Let me just get out of your way." Carlton slipped away from the computer and sidled toward the lab door. He paused to glance back and smile. "Have a great rest of the day."

"You too," Kramer called.

When Carlton was gone, Kramer studied the computer. In a way he felt violated.

No, this can't be a coincidence. Carlton is up to something.

You were trying to find something important, Carlton. But you didn't find anything, did you?

Kramer took his seat and e-mailed Garrett right away:

> Garrett,
>
> I hope I'm not overreacting, but I wanted you to know that I came to work early and found Carlton on my computer. He said he was just doing updates, which is possible, but he acted as if I'd caught him in the middle of something when I showed up. You know me;

I'm very protective of our "stuff." Anyway, I just wanted you to know to make sure that's what he was supposed to be doing.

Now that I think about it, with Carlton being head of the IT department, he can probably read this, too. ☺ Oh well.

Thanks,

Kramer

CHAPTER 6

Listening

On Wednesday morning, Garrett's phone rang. It was Kramer.

"Got time to drop by the lab?" Kramer asked.

Garrett glanced at his to-do list and rolled his eyes. "Is it important?"

"Yeah, I think you should come over here right away."

It took Garrett only a few minutes to reach the lab, where Kramer was pacing back and forth. Garrett wondered if this had something to do with the e-mail about Carlton.

"Garrett, please have a seat."

Garrett complied and wondered why Kramer was being so mysterious.

Kramer stopped pacing, elation glowing in his eyes. Garrett had never seen him so jubilant.

"Garrett, you know I've been working hard to figure out how to replenish the glutathione in B228."

"Yes."

"Well, it's working! We're getting these chemical reactions to take place, and we have these extra electrons."

Garrett digested this information in silence, unsure where Kramer was going with this.

Kramer sat down across from him. His hands were shaking. "The free radicals are being killed. We've done it, Garrett! We've done it. B228 will fight cancer!"

Garrett stared at him. "You mean help *prevent* cancer."

"Well, yeah, that too. But it looks like these types of reactions should fight existing cells as well!"

Garrett leaned back in his chair, letting the news sink in. He struggled to breathe. The ramifications of what Kramer had said slammed into him like a Mack truck. Could it really be true? He thought about all those struggling cancer patients who needed help. The possibilities were staggering.

Of course, an independent third party would need to confirm their findings. And they most likely had a long way to go to perfect the product before it would be available on the market. But getting to this point had been the biggest hurdle to overcome.

Garrett stood up and patted Kramer on the shoulder, barely able to contain his elation. "This is a colossal accomplishment. You should be very proud."

"You know this was a team effort, Garrett. It wasn't just me." He frowned. "But I can't help but wonder what kind of reception this product will get in the medical field."

"I don't wonder. Our products are often viewed negatively by the medical establishments because they're untraditional—not to mention inexpensive. It's just not the form they would expect something like this to come in. It may not be accepted well at all, but let's not be discouraged from doing our mission. People need this product, and if we can provide it, that's what counts."

Garrett considered the next steps that needed to be taken. Thoughts were hitting him so quickly, he could hardly process them. His temples throbbed.

He knew one thing—they needed to protect this information for B228 so no one could steal it.

Garrett lowered his voice. "Kramer, we need to keep this information to ourselves right now. I'll let the management team know a little, but not much."

"You know where I store the information, right?"

Garrett nodded. "Yeah. Let's be sure no one else does."

On Thursday morning, Garrett awoke in a Detroit hotel, his head throbbing. He hadn't slept well and wanted to be in top form for the breakfast meeting he'd scheduled with his father in the hotel lobby at 9:00 a.m. Maybe a shower would help.

On his way to the bathroom, Garrett combed his fingers through his wild bedhead hair and drew in a deep breath. His anxious mind flailed through a tangle of thoughts and emotions.

What would his father be like? Would he like his father, and would his father like him? After all, being related by blood didn't guarantee likability. His stomach churned.

After the shower, he sat at the desk and jotted down questions he didn't want to forget to ask. In the elevator he watched the red digital number count down the floors. He rubbed his sweaty palms on his slacks. It was a countdown to one of the most important meetings of his life.

3. 2. 1.

He took a deep breath.

Okay, this is it.

Before he stepped off the elevator, he said a quick prayer, which made him feel a little more at ease. As he walked in the direction of the front desk, where he'd agreed to meet his father, he wondered what his dad would look like. Would he be tall or short? Would he look like him?

The instant he saw the man standing at the desk, he knew it was Tom, his father. He recognized the same high forehead, the same cleft chin, the same black hair that his own mirror always reflected. The main difference was that his father's face was a much older reflection of Garrett, with salt and pepper hair and a face deeply lined as if he spent too much time in the sun.

Too many unanswered questions roiled inside for him to feel comfortable greeting his father with a hug, so they made friendly eye contact and shook hands instead. Tears trickled down his father's face.

While his father struggled to regain his composure, they found a seat in the dining room. For a moment, uncomfortable silence filled the space between them. Garrett had rehearsed what to say, but now he could barely think. With trembling hands, he unfolded the paper with the questions, but now he wondered if he should ask them. What should he say to the father who abandoned him forty years ago?

He met his father's gaze, amazed at how alike they were. "I have your nose," he said.

"And your mother's blue eyes." Tom dabbed his eyes with a napkin.

"It's good to see you."

"Good to see you too. I'm sorry it took so long."

Another awkward pause. Tom blew his nose.

The waitress came and took their orders. Garrett could hardly think about food—his stomach felt sick—but he ordered anyhow. After she left, Tom said, "Go ahead. You must have a lot of questions for me."

Garrett hesitated, studied the questions on the paper, then pushed the paper aside. Tom was already emotional, and the questions he wanted—no, needed—to ask weren't easy ones to answer.

Might as well just get everything out in the open.

Garrett took a deep breath. "Okay, I'll start with the toughie first. Why didn't you want me?"

Tom had just dried his eyes, but they brimmed with tears again. "Garrett, I didn't want to give you to someone else. Please believe me. Your mother and I were very young, but we were so looking forward to your birth and to holding you in our arms."

Something the size of a baseball got stuck in Garrett's throat.

"During your delivery, there were complications, and your mom . . ." Tom glanced down at his empty plate, chin trembling. Finally, he met Garrett's eyes. "I'm afraid she passed away."

Garrett glanced away, eyes moistening. His mother was dead. The thought slammed into him, leaving him feeling stunned and lost. He'd hoped to meet her, but now that could never be.

She'll never meet her grandkids.

Their food arrived, but Garrett doubted he could eat anything.

Seconds ticked by as Tom tried to get his emotions back under control. Garrett needed the moment too.

Tom wiped his eyes again. "It was really tough because I didn't have much family, and I had to take care of you by myself."

Garrett closed his eyes. He knew where this conversation was going.

"I loved you so much, Garrett, but I couldn't care for

you . . . not the way you needed or deserved. Not by myself. Not when I had a job. Garrett, you're the only child I ever had."

Garrett opened his eyes and studied the careworn face, trying to understand.

"I let someone else have you because I loved you so much. I thought you could do so much better in life if you were with a good family." He smiled through his tears. "I guess I was right. I mean, look at you."

Garrett sighed and wiped his eyes. For how many years had he struggled with bitterness, thinking his parents hadn't loved him?

When he looked into his father's eyes and saw the sadness there because of the tough choice he'd had to make—and then to see the love he still had for him, even after all these years—something broke inside. Maybe it was love knocking those stubborn walls of bitterness down.

His birth parents *had* loved him. They'd wanted to keep him. And they probably would have if—

Emotions overwhelmed him, and his eyes filled his tears. He glanced away.

Tom reached across the table and grabbed his son's hand. "Garrett, could you please forgive me for all the pain this may have caused you?"

Garrett squeezed his father's hand back. Then he grabbed a napkin and wiped his eyes. "Yes, Tom—Dad—I forgive you." He paused a moment to take a deep breath. "What you did is hard for me to understand, but meeting you and hearing you speak about it helps me understand a little bit better. I do have good parents, and they gave me a great environment to grow up in."

Garrett cleared his throat. "But now. To finally see you after all these years. To know you didn't want to give me away. I can't describe how much this means to me."

They spent the next couple of hours talking about their lives. Tom had worked in Detroit car factories his whole life, but he was now retired. He'd remarried later in life.

Garrett told his father about his life, his family, and Nexus. They talked a lot about Garrett's real mother—about what she was like and what she'd represented.

They both agreed to start over and begin a new relationship together. Garrett offered to give his father a tour of Nexus and wanted to introduce him to the family. Tom said he could hardly wait. They'd schedule a time.

At the airport that evening, Garrett hugged his father goodbye for the first time and flew home with a tremendous sense of relief. The big question about his birth parents finally had an answer.

Margret would have a lot of questions for him—he couldn't wait to talk to her.

As Garrett arrived at the office on Friday morning, he thought about his wife's birthday on Saturday. He'd organized a surprise party for her but hadn't found adequate time to finalize some of the details. He'd been working too much lately, and their relationship had suffered as a result.

As he glanced at her portrait perched on his desk, he thought about how much he loved her. He could hardly wait to celebrate her birthday.

After spending an hour on party plans, Garrett ran over to the local potter to pick up the special piece of pottery he'd requested for Margret. She enjoyed original gifts, not the cookie-cutter variety. Ordering such gifts took more effort on his part, but he enjoyed seeing the delight on her face when she opened them.

That afternoon, someone rapped on Garrett's open door.

Garrett glanced toward the door. "Come on in, John."

"Garrett, can I talk to you about something that's not related to work?"

"Sure. No problem." Garrett gestured to a chair.

John's face was flushed, his eyes red. Had he been crying?

"John, what is it? What's wrong?"

"Remember when I told you about my son, Sam? He's been hanging out with the wrong crowd." He shrugged. "I don't know. I guess he's searching for something."

"Of course, I remember."

"Well, I've got a really bad feeling about this weekend." John's voice cracked with emotion. "I confronted him last night. I meant well, but it didn't go well at all. I'm sure I didn't handle it as well as I should have."

Garrett was tempted to ask questions or give input, but maybe what John needed most was someone to listen.

"Garrett, before he stormed out of my house, he said I won't ever see him again. I don't know what that means, but I'm really scared about this weekend. I don't know if he's going to try to hurt himself or if he just never wants to see me again." A tear streaked down John's cheek.

Garrett had always seen John as the tough outdoorsman, ready to hunt the next buck, so to see him so emotional wasn't easy. He didn't seem like the John he knew.

Sometimes life just seems so hard.

"John, I'm so sorry. You know Nexus is kind of like family to me. I'll do anything I can to help you. In fact, if you want to leave work early, you are free to go. I'll understand."

"Thanks, Garrett. I'm sorry to burden you with my problems. I don't really have a lot of family living in the area anymore, so I don't feel like I have a lot of people to turn to right now."

John got up from his chair and moved toward the door.

Garrett thought of something else. "John, try not to worry too much. I'm sure those words were said in the heat of the moment and aren't a true indication of Sam's feelings. I'll keep both of you in my prayers. I know this is a big burden, but hopefully things will turn out for the best."

CHAPTER 7

Investing

As Garrett hoped, Margret's birthday party, shared with thirty family members and closest friends, was a huge surprise. Garrett had prepared a special song for the occasion, and Carter and Jasmine sang while he accompanied them on the piano. Margret was touched by the performance, hand pressed to her face and tears glistening in her eyes.

Close to nine, when everyone was enjoying a group game together, Garrett received a text from John.

Sam is in trouble. Call me.

He'd never received a text from John before—maybe his conversation about trying to better relate to Gen Y employees was sinking in. He wondered what was wrong. Had Sam hurt himself as John feared?

Garrett glanced up from the phone. Margret was watching him from across the room, a question in her eyes. It wasn't the ideal time to be making a phone call. He sent a text back.

OK, in a few.

Twenty minutes later, the group game was over. Everybody was relaxing in the living room and chatting. Garrett slipped into the kitchen to make the call.

"John, what's happening?"

John's voice quavered. "Sam's in the hospital."

"Oh, no. What happened?"

"Drug overdose. Got a call from the paramedics as they were taking him to the hospital. He's in critical condition." John paused before choking out, "The doctors are hoping he'll make it through the night."

Garrett closed his eyes, hand to his head. This was not good.

Then to top it all off, he glanced out the kitchen door. Margret was watching him again, her mouth a tight seam of disapproval. But surely she would understand once he explained.

He looked away. "John, what hospital?"

"Memorial."

"All right. I'll see you soon."

By ten o'clock, all the guests had left, and there was a lot of cleanup to do. Garrett decided it was a good time to explain John's situation, but Margret beat him to the punch.

"Garrett, who were you talking to on the phone tonight?" She stood at the kitchen sink, rinsing off dishes before stacking them in the dishwasher.

He told her about the call.

The corners of her eyes wrinkled in concern. "Is Sam's condition serious?"

"He's in critical condition," John said. "So, yeah, I'd say it's pretty serious." He paused. "I really think I should head over there and be with John."

She stared at him, anger choking her voice. "Tonight?" When he didn't respond quickly enough, she turned back to the sink and grabbed a plate as if about to break it over his head. "Well, I guess I'll be cleaning up the mess from my *own* birthday party by myself!"

Garrett touched her back and forced himself to be patient. "Margret, just leave the mess. I'll clean it up tomorrow. I promise."

She looked at him as if she didn't believe him. "Garrett—"

"You know you're the most important person in my life. I really tried to make this a special night for you, but John's son might *die*. I need to show him my support too."

Margret sighed and gave him a slow nod. Though his absence would put a damper on the evening, she understood. "It's fine. Go ahead. I understand." Her voice sounded distinctly unenthusiastic.

He kissed her on the forehead and went to get his keys.

When Garrett saw John, he knew his choice had been the right one. John's eyes were red from crying, and he looked unshaved and unkempt—unusual for John. He barely seemed like the John that Garrett knew.

John motioned to the hospital bed, where his pale son lay amid a tangle of tubes and monitors. Garrett accepted a chair, and John returned to his seat beside his son. He grabbed a tissue to mop up fresh tears.

"I can't tell you how much it means to have you here." Sadness choked his voice.

"I'm sorry I couldn't come sooner." Garrett chose not

to mention the birthday party. He didn't want John to feel bad that Garrett had sacrificed the rest of the evening with his wife.

Garrett studied Sam. He didn't know what death looked like, but if looks were any indication, Sam had to be close. "How's he doing?"

John shrugged and shook his head. "He's stable, at least. The doc says we'll know by morning."

In other words, a long night lay ahead. A somber vigil.

Silence filled the space between them. Garrett wasn't sure what to say. Finally, he suggested that they pray for Sam, which they both did aloud. Then they talked about work and life and whatever came to mind until the wee hours of the morning. Coffee and worry kept them awake.

"I can't believe you've stayed here all night with me." John rubbed his weary face. "You didn't have to do that."

Garrett shrugged.

"I knew you were a thoughtful boss, Garrett, but I didn't expect this."

"I hope you'll think of me as more than your boss, John. I care about you and your son."

Around 4:00 a.m., the doctor dropped by and checked on Sam's vitals. What they'd been hoping for finally flashed across the doctor's face in the form of a smile. "The worst is over. I think your son is going to pull through."

Garrett reached for the tissue box because John needed it again.

After the doctor left, John said, "If you're as tired as I am, you should probably head home. Besides, your family will be wondering where you are."

Garrett didn't say anything. He thought of Margret lying in bed without him at her side.

"Seriously, Garrett. You should head home and get some sleep."

Garrett nodded. Sam was going to make it—that meant John was going to be okay too. He rose. "Text me if anything changes."

"I will."

As Garrett crossed the empty parking lot to his car, he wondered how he would hold up if one of his kids ever overdosed. Just the thought of possibly losing his son—as if he and John had switched places—made his throat tighten and his eyes burn.

That must be how Tom felt when he had to give me away to

strangers. Imagine having to give up someone you love so much. Your own flesh and blood.

He could barely comprehend it.

He slipped into the quiet house. Everyone was surely still asleep. To be certain, he peeked in on his kids, his heart swelling to see them alive and well. Untouched by the evils of drugs. A profound peace settled on him just to see them safe and healthy.

When he slipped into bed around four thirty, Margret rolled over and embraced him.

"Oh, you're awake." He snuggled close and kissed her hair.

"I've barely slept. Not with you gone."

"Well, now you can sleep. We both can. Sam is going to make it."

She sighed. "I'm sorry about last night. You worked so hard to pull off that great party, and I was pretty grumpy when you decided to go to the hospital."

"Forgiven and forgotten."

He was so glad she wasn't still mad at him. After a yawn, he drifted off.

On Monday afternoon, Garrett dropped by Carlton's office for a scheduled meeting. After they went over the typical IT agenda, Garrett remembered Kramer's e-mail about finding Carlton working on his computer. He liked to have a good understanding of his employee's jobs, and the e-mail had sparked his curiosity.

"I understand that sometimes you come in early to work on individual work stations," he said. "What are your specific duties when you do this?"

A wounded look glinted in Carlton's icy-blue eyes. "Why do you ask?"

Garrett shrugged. "Well, it's my responsibility to lead the organization, and I like to have knowledge of all our activities."

Carlton folded arms across his beefy chest and avoided eye contact. His silence spoke volumes.

"I'm not trying to micromanage you, Carlton. I have more than enough to do as it is. But I'm just wondering about your specific tasks these days."

Carlton shifted uncomfortably in his seat. He finally looked at Garrett. "Most of the time, I'm just applying upgrades to protect our computers from viruses. There are some really nasty viruses out there. They could mess up our productivity if I'm not doing my job."

Garrett nodded. "Thanks. You know that I appreciate all you do. Maybe I don't say it enough, but I'm saying it now."

Carlton met his eyes and smiled. "Thanks."

After returning to his office, Garrett reviewed his conversation with Carlton. Something beyond Carlton's defensiveness bugged him, like a shred of meat trapped between two molars.

Was Carlton really just doing virus updates? Or was he snooping around, looking for important company information?

He freely admitted to wanting to learn as much about the business as possible. Was he trying to find information about the B228 project? What might he plan to do with such information if found?

There's one way to find out.

After giving it some thought, Garrett called his computer consulting company and requested information about how to check his employees' e-mail accounts. To keep his inquiry private from Carlton and others, he talked to the company's owner. Next, he double-checked the Nexus employee manual and found the policy statement in question; the manual guaranteed that Nexus had the ability and right to review employees' e-mails at any time for any reason. Looking through Carlton's work e-mail account for clues about his behavior would take some time, so Garrett decided to put off the task for later.

On Tuesday, Garrett left with Derek to attend a trade show in Chicago. It had been a while since the last time he accompanied Derek on a sales trip like this. By Wednesday they were on the floor, trying to sell all the products Nexus had to offer.

For a few minutes Garrett sat back and watched Derek, the salesman, in action. He was impressed. Derek knew how to work the crowd, and the way he educated potential vendors about their products encouraged him.

After a long day of working together at the trade show, they headed to a favorite Mexican restaurant for dinner. The restaurant was busy and the noise level high. Derek and Garrett ordered and discussed the day's activities while enjoying chips and salsa.

Garrett squeezed a fresh lemon slice over his ice water, took a sip, and then spoke. "Derek, I want you to know that I think you do a nice job with the customers you work with. You've got a natural gift of being able to connect with them, presenting them with the information, and closing the sale."

Derek smiled, hazel eyes twinkling. "Thanks for saying so. I really enjoy it, and I'm thankful for the support and tools you give me to do my job. Those really help."

Garrett remembered Erin's e-mail about Derek's encounter with Kari of the marketing department. "Funny you should say that. Tell me this. Do you feel like you're getting everything you need from the office to be successful out here in the sales field?"

Derek scooped some thick and spicy salsa onto a tortilla chip and thought for a moment. "You know, one area has been a little shaky lately."

"Really. What area is that?"

"Well, to be frank, I don't have the greatest trust in our marketing department. Kari's a great person, but sometimes she seems overly preoccupied with other things going on in her life. I'm not sure she realizes how important our sales materials are, especially when it comes to timelines. So I'm constantly badgering her about timelines, and it feels like I'm bothering her."

Garrett nodded. "I understand you've had some frustrations with that department."

"That's putting it mildly." Salsa dripped from the chip to the table as Derek bit into it.

"I'd like to work with you and Kari on this issue, and I'd like to challenge you to handle every situation the best you can. It takes a lot of patience anytime we have this many people working together and depending on each other. There's no question that we're better as a team than we are individually, so we'll have to figure this out."

"Patience isn't usually something I have a lot of." Derek ran thick fingers over his blond crew cut.

Garrett wondered if he could get Derek to open up about himself a little more. "Did you say *trust* isn't something you have a lot of?"

"No, I said *patience*, but trust is probably something else I lack too. You know, Garrett, that's probably why I haven't had much luck dating anyone long term." He shrugged and took a sip of his cola. "I mean, who wants to spend time with somebody who doesn't trust people and doesn't have very much patience?"

Garrett studied Derek. *At least he realizes his own weaknesses. That's the first step if anyone wants to improve.*

Garrett cleared his throat. "Derek, just because your real family let you down in some areas doesn't mean I or others at Nexus will."

Derek said nothing. He stirred his soft drink with his straw, eyes on his ice cubes.

"I want you to reach your full potential. Not being able to trust people or have patience with them might restrict you from contributing all you could to our team."

Derek nodded slowly. "I guess you're right."

"Leaders can't make excuses about why they're coming up short in some areas; they have to grow and develop those areas."

Derek remained silent, eyes still on his drink.

"I know you think you're just a sales guy, but you're head of the Sales department, and your employees look up to you."

Derek was quiet. Too quiet.

Garrett wondered if Derek thought he was being too hard on him. "Sorry. I didn't mean to lecture you."

Finally, Derek lifted his eyes to Garrett's face. "No, it's all right. I appreciate the way you're always encouraging me to grow in my leadership skills and building me and others up. Because you're always investing in us, your employees, we're open to your advice when you let us know how we can improve."

Garrett spread his hands. "Well, I try."

"I understand what you're trying to tell me. I have total confidence when I'm in the sales arena. When it comes to other areas of the business, though, well . . ."—he shrugged—"sometimes you have more belief in me than I do in myself."

Garrett decided to finish the conversation on a positive note. "I think your potential is great. I hope our company continues to grow, and I want you to be equipped to grow with it."

By the time the server brought their entrees, the chips were gone. Garrett practically drooled over his cast iron platter of sizzling steak fajitas.

"I guess it's no understatement to say you love Mexican food." Derek chuckled.

Garrett nodded as he took a warm flour tortilla and began to layer meat, peppers, and onions on it. "I never miss this place when I'm in Chicago."

They both dug in, and Garrett wasn't disappointed. As they ate, their conversation went in a direction he hadn't foreseen.

"Garrett, I'm glad you came on this road trip with me. It's nice to have someone to hang out with after the show."

"So, what do you normally do when I'm not here? Don't you hang out with the other guys from the show?"

"Sometimes. But that's a different crowd, and most of the stuff they like to do . . . well, it leaves me feeling not so great about myself afterwards."

"Why? What do they do?"

Derek lowered his eyes and voice. "They hit the bars and strip clubs."

Garrett couldn't hide his grimace.

"You never participate in that type of stuff," Derek said. "What's up with that?"

It was refreshing the way Derek was opening up to him about this area of his life. Garrett welcomed the opportunity to share his views. "I guess I've seen the more destructive side of that type of behavior." He paused. "I'm not saying certain activities are necessarily wrong; it's just a very slippery slope if you get started down that path."

"It's your family, isn't it?"

Garrett nodded. "Yeah. I really value my wife and kids. I wouldn't want Margret participating in that lifestyle, so I guess I've chosen not to as well."

Derek finished one of his burritos and paused to wipe his mouth with his napkin. "But aren't you tempted at all to participate with the other guys tonight?"

Garrett considered. *Now how do I get my next point across without making Derek feel condemned?* "I guess everybody faces temptations in their lives, and we're not always successful at saying no. Are we?"

Derek shook his head as he chewed his food.

"But I represent my family *and* Nexus when I'm in public," Garrett said. "It's important to me to be a good ambassador. Derek, you represent Nexus, not just yourself, when you're on the road. I think you understand what I'm talking about."

Derek nodded. "Participating in certain activities could make Nexus look bad. That's a good reminder."

During the rest of dinner they talked about Garrett's meeting with his real father and how it had impacted his life. As they chatted, Garrett realized that, in a way, Derek was fatherless.

He looks to me to be that father figure. Wow. What a responsibility!

CHAPTER 8

Micromanagement

On Friday, Garrett was back in the office. During a meeting with John, they discussed inefficiencies in packaging the arthritis cream. It was taking too long to get the product packaged, so they brainstormed ways to fix the problem. Eventually, it became obvious to Garrett that he and John weren't going to agree on a solution. Knowing John's personality, Garrett decided it wouldn't be good to force his ideas at this time.

"John, I can tell you feel strongly about your idea to fix this problem. How long do you think it would take your plan to work and produce results?"

"One week, tops."

"Fine. How about we implement your plan right away? We can introduce it together on Monday. Then we'll give it a week or so. If we don't like the results, we can switch over and see if my recommended plan works better."

Later, alone in his office, Garrett rose and stared out the window at the parking lot while he sipped a fresh mug of coffee.

I don't want to micromanage John, but I'll fall off my chair if his plan has any chance of working.

Then he remembered something he'd once heard. Sometimes the right step is to let your employees make a wrong decision and fail. Learning from their mistakes can sometimes have more impact than guiding them away from their mistakes.

By the day's end, Garrett could hardly wait to go home.

"Got big plans?" Julissa asked brightly after he turned off his office lights and closed the door.

He smiled. "Sure do. Margret and I are taking the kids on a weekend getaway to a water park and resort."

"Oh, that sounds like fun." Julissa smiled as she tidied up her desk.

"The kids have been looking forward to this for weeks."

"What about you and Margret?"

"We're looking forward to it, too. It's been a stressful last few weeks."

Julissa shook her head. "I can't imagine. Meeting your father for the first time. Well, have fun!"

On the way home, Garrett's foot was heavier on the gas pedal than usual. Thirty minutes later, the car was packed, and they were off. When they arrived at the resort, the kids were so excited they could hardly control themselves.

"Now just calm down," Margret said as Garrett checked in. "We have to get settled in our rooms first."

"Um, Mom. Surprise!" Carter unzipped his pants to reveal his swimming trunks underneath. "I thought this would save time."

Jasmine had done the same thing with her swimsuit. "Can we go swimming now?" she asked. "Please?"

"Sure." Garrett chuckled. "Why not? We can always unpack later."

Garrett and Margret headed to the indoor water park and dropped the kids off at the kids care center, where activities and child care were included. Then he led his lovely wife to the nicest restaurant at the resort, where they found a quiet corner with lit candles, white-linen napkins, and romantic music playing over the speakers.

A petite waitress with frizzy brown hair took their drink orders with a smile and left them to study their menus.

Garrett leaned back, already feeling the tension in his shoulders starting to slip away.

"At last. Some time to ourselves." Margret smiled at him, then studied her menu. "In the next twenty-four hours, hopefully the only reason the kids will get out of the pool is to sleep or eat."

"Exactly. More time to have you to myself."

Margret eyed Garrett flirtatiously.

"It's nice to be here and spend extra time as a family," Garrett said. "But I must admit that I also treasure these times alone with you."

Margret reached across the table and squeezed his hand, eyes twinkling.

For a while they reminisced about their past together and talked about dreams for their lives, their kids, and Nexus over the next few years. He concluded with, "It's been a stressful last few weeks. In fact, last week was so crazy with the road trip to Chicago and other things that I haven't updated you on Kramer's progress in research and development."

"Well, since I *am* on the board of directors, I certainly like to keep up with the latest news."

"Especially news that could affect our stocks."

Her eyes danced. "Well, we *are* the only stockholders in the company, Garrett. If things are going to go south, I'd certainly like to know in advance, if that's possible."

"No, it's nothing like that. I have only good news—in fact, the best. I promise."

She smiled and brushed back brown locks that framed her oval face and prominent cheek bones. "Now that's what I like to hear."

The waitress returned with their drinks and salads, and then took their orders.

After she left, Garrett sipped his sweetened raspberry tea. "I think some of our goals at Nexus are finally becoming a reality. Kramer has developed the B228 to kill free radicals, which means it will effectively not only prevent cancer—but also fight it."

Margret almost dropped her fork. "Are you kidding me?" She pressed a hand to her heart. "I mean, I knew you and Kramer had been exploring the possibilities of such a product for some time, but I frankly wasn't sure you'd ever reach this point."

"Oh ye of little faith." He grinned.

She dropped her voice almost to a whisper, as if the restaurant were swarming with spies. "Do you realize how huge this development is? Do you have any idea—?"

"Yeah, I do." He munched on his salad and savored the rich, tangy dressing.

She used her napkin to fan herself, her face slightly pale.

He reached for her hand. "Are you okay?"

"I'm not sure how to handle this. I mean"—she leaned toward him as if not wanting to be overheard—"a product that *fights cancer*? Do you realize what this means?"

"Yeah, our stocks will go through the roof." He quickly added, "But money, as you know, has never been important to me. I'm not that shallow. I'd rather think about all the sick people we'll be able to help."

"Garrett, this product will save lives." She paused for emphasis, her eyes wide. "If Nexus pulls this off, you could win the Nobel Prize."

Garrett chuckled and waved off her words. "Well, I'm not willing to think that grand just yet. We still have a lot of work to do before the product ever hits the market. It's been very expensive to develop."

"But well worth the investment, it sounds like. Will the product be available in drink form?"

He shrugged. "We haven't really gotten that far yet. I lean toward a supplement, but we've never done supplements before, and that would be a new venture. I'll let you know how it goes."

"Please do. I want to know everything. This is huge." She paused. "I probably don't need to say this, but you do have the product data under lock and key, I trust."

"Yes, it's in a safe place. Not even our IT department can access it."

"Really. Well, where is it?"

He gave her a few hints.

Their meals arrived. Garrett tasted his steak. Pure heaven.

"There are a couple of other things I'd like to talk to you about too," he said.

Margret tasted her Cornish hen and closed her eyes with delight. "Wow. This is superb. Oh, I'm sorry. Go ahead."

"You know, we've wanted to add some outside directors to the board for a while now. I have a couple of candidates I think would be great. When we get back to Monroe, I'd like you to review their credentials."

Was it his imagination, or did he sense hesitation in her reply?

She wiped her mouth and seemed to choose her words carefully. "Since you and I have been the only board members, adding others who are not part of our family is a big deal to me."

"Of course."

"But I also realize the need to do this. How long can we carry this load by ourselves? Do you think we need to add the new board members right away?"

After savoring another slice of steak, he sipped his tea. "I do. The company is growing so fast. And once we've developed B228, the company could grow even faster. Having other minds to help us with future decisions and direction would be valuable."

"Okay, fine, if you really think so." She sipped her lemon water, clearly not thrilled about the idea but willing to acquiesce. "Is there other Nexus business you wanted to discuss?"

Garrett tensed. They'd never discussed the next idea before, and she was more timid about big changes than he was. "I have a new idea for Nexus. I'd like us to think about offering the management team a stock options program."

She stared at him. "Why would you want to do that?"

Garrett set his fork down and chose his words carefully. "Well, for a few reasons. I think if some of the employees actually owned part of the company, they'd treat Nexus differently—not as employees but as owners. This could have a huge impact on how they work, what kind of decisions they make. And it would motivate them because if the company does well, their stock price would go up. I think they would also watch expenses and the profit/loss statement with a different attitude."

Her expression said it all: she wasn't ready for this, at least not yet.

"Garrett, I love how you think, and I care about Nexus and your employees and people in general. But I think . . ." She sighed. "I think I need more time to consider your idea. I might even have some questions later."

"No problem. Take as long as you need."

"I knew you'd understand." She smiled. "So . . . how about we order dessert?"

Across the room, a blonde sitting alone turned her gaze away from Garrett and Margret and wiped her mouth on her napkin as her waiter approached. After ordering dessert, she rose and sauntered to the lobby, where she pulled out her smartphone and pressed "redial."

A man's voice picked up. "So, how did it go?"

"Great. They just ordered dessert."

"How did you know that? I'm impressed."

"I told you I was a professional lip reader. Did you

think I was lying?"

"No. I just—"

"Never mind."

"So what did they say? Anything of interest?"

"Oh yeah. Plenty about a product called B228. You'll want to know about this."

"Tell me."

So she did.

He said, "I see that your services have been worth every penny."

"I better get back. They seem to be doing family chit-chat now, but you never know. They might tell me more. I'll be in touch if I learn anything else."

"The money will be in your account in a half hour." He paused. "Oh, and remember. Part of your fee includes confidentiality. I'm sure you understand the importance of that, especially in this situation."

She chuckled. "Absolutely. Their lips aren't sealed. But mine definitely are."

CHAPTER 9

Change

"Hope your weekend getaway with the kids went well," Julissa said as Garrett strolled into the office on Monday morning. Marianne was taking a few weeks off to visit her sick mother.

"It was terrific. Thanks for asking. How was yours?"

"I had a date." Julissa blushed and busied herself with straightening her paper clip holder.

"Anybody I know?"

"No."

"Nice guy?"

She nodded. "The best."

"He better be, or I'll call him into my office for a long talk."

She laughed. "I'll be sure to tell him that."

At his desk, Garrett checked his e-mail. There was a new message from his dad:

Hey, Garrett. I can hardly wait to see where you work. See you this afternoon. I'm looking forward to the tour. Love you. Dad.

Based on the e-mail address, Garrett knew which "Dad" it was. His throat tightened.

Wow. What a weird feeling to be in touch with his birth father after all these years.

While making his usual Monday morning tour of the plant, Garrett ran into John.

"Garrett, I wanted to ask you something. Remember me telling you about my grandson, Brandon, the base-ball player?"

"Sure, the home run hitter. The next Babe Ruth. Of course."

"Well, his team's in a baseball tournament, and the championship is tomorrow in Charlotte." John glanced down, his tone apologetic. "I know it's short notice, but I wondered . . . Would you mind if I took the day off and attended his game? I know we have a couple of meetings planned, but it would mean a lot to him if I could skip those and see him play."

"John, of course you can go to his game. I wouldn't have it any other way."

Next, Garrett moved around the plant, trying to chat with as many employees as he could before the management team meeting, which began promptly at 9:00 a.m.

Garrett started the meeting in his normal fashion by asking his staff to share about their weekends. Then they moved right into individual department updates. During John's turn, he reported that he'd decided to terminate an employee who wasn't performing up to expectations but then changed his mind.

"When I brought the employee into my office, I decided to try and salvage the relationship," John said. "I tried this coaching thing Garrett has been working on with me. I'm pleasantly surprised by how the employee responded to the situation. As of now, he's still employed here at Nexus."

Garrett nodded and clapped John on the shoulder, so pleased that John was working hard to modify his management style.

And hey, we also didn't have to fire another employee.

Kramer's update was next. "One new project might sound a little weird. We're working to design a biodegradable jar. We haven't perfected it yet, but we're getting closer."

"That's very exciting," Derek said with a boyish grin. "Our customers are looking for this type of thing. Plastic and glass bottles are tough on the landfills. I think this'll really help sell our products."

Garrett had mixed emotions but kept his thoughts to himself. Of course, he wanted Nexus to be green too, but it was easier for employees, rather than the owner, to get excited about innovations in green products. Bottom line: he was worried about the expense. He jotted himself a note to discuss costs with Kramer later.

Garrett used the last fifteen minutes of the meeting to have the group formulate some sales, material, and labor percentage goals for the next quarter. Sometimes he liked to raise their expectations of what they thought they could accomplish as a team.

With the meeting behind them, Garrett invited Kari and Derek to lunch at a casual restaurant only a half mile from Nexus. They found seats and placed their orders. As soon as the waitress left, Garrett addressed some of the concerns Derek had expressed after the trade show in Chicago. By having the discussion over lunch, Garrett thought the conversation would be more relaxed.

He was right. The conversation about communication, timelines, and expectations went well. Unlike a lot of situations, Garrett found himself doing most of the talking. He'd been educated about the situation and wanted to make sure they understood his message and expectations for resolving the conflict.

After lunch, Garrett sent Derek and Kari back to the office in the car because he wanted to walk back and get some exercise. During his stroll, he reflected on the organization and his role.

Every once in a while, it just feels lonely at the top.

He prided himself in running an organization that functioned not from the top down but more horizontally. Nonetheless, his position at the top sometimes put him in an awkward spot; there was no one inside the organization he could vent his frustrations to or confide in. He lacked that leader who could pat him on the back for the good work he did.

Stop feeling sorry for yourself. You know that much of your reward is in the fulfillment of your mission. If products are helping people, isn't that rewarding enough?

As he drew closer to the building, he reminded himself of the great people he got to work with every day and how much he enjoyed going to work.

His mind drifted to the Carlton situation.

I really should talk to Erin about this.

Inside, he strolled toward the employee lounge to put his lunch leftovers in the refrigerator. As he entered the room and headed toward the refrigerator, his head jerked toward the corner. Sally Meyers, one of John's production employees, was sitting and talking on her cell phone.

When she saw Garrett, she hung up, her face streaked with tears. Sally was in her fifties; her brown hair had turned iron gray.

"Sally, is everything okay?"

Sally bit her lip as if unsure what to say. Finally: "I wanted to go to Grandparents Day at my grandson's school on Friday, but I can't. I was just telling my daughter I wouldn't be able to make it."

"Grandparents Day is important. Why can't you go?"

Sally pulled out a tissue and dabbed at her mascara streaks. "I didn't put in my request early enough. John said I have to work."

Hmm. Seems like John had a similar request recently. Smells like a double standard to me.

"Did you tell John why you needed time off? I'm sure he'd let you go if he knew what the event was."

"Yes, I told him. He said I have to follow the rules like everyone else and that he can't make exceptions. I told him I just found out about it, but he wouldn't change his mind. I understand. He wants to teach us to follow the rules. It's okay."

No, it's not okay.

The memory of John's request to attend his grandson's baseball game irked him. Back in his office, Garrett called John. "John, I just had an interesting conversation with Sally Meyers in the break room."

A pause. "Okay. What's this about, Garrett?"

"She asked if she could go to Grandparents Day at her grandson's school, and you said no." Although he kept his voice even, Garrett was certain John could hear the steam behind them.

"She didn't put the request in until today," John said, his tone wary. "I have a policy of two weeks' prior notice on all requests. If I break the rules for her, everything will be in disorder."

Garrett gripped his phone tighter. All the training he'd done with John on how to treat people better seemed to be in vain.

He just doesn't get it.

"Maybe I should have the same policy for you, John,"

he said. "Maybe you need to skip that baseball game tomorrow." Garrett knew John wouldn't miss the double standard.

Another pause. "I'm sorry, Garrett. You're right." He sighed. "I feel really bad, and I think I hurt Sally too. She's a really good person. Never requests much time off. And she's one of my best workers. I guess I made a one-size-fits-all rule because of a few employees who make requests all the time."

He paused, and Garrett waited.

"Garrett, I'll make this right. I'll talk to Sally and make sure she gets to Grandparents Day. I'll stay and work tomorrow too. I feel bad about this."

Garrett felt himself cooling off. "No, John. I want you to go to the baseball game tomorrow, but I just wanted to make sure you got my point."

"I got it, Garrett. I do."

"I'm glad to hear it."

After lunch, Garrett welcomed his dad, Tom, at the entrance and gave him a grand tour of the facility. "I'm so glad you could fit the tour into your schedule, Dad."

Tom's face seemed to brighten at Garrett's use of the word *Dad*. He clapped Garrett on the shoulder, his eyes taking in the chrome and steel of the lobby. "Wow, this is some place! And my son gets to work here every day."

That's right. Tom had worked in car factories most of his working life. A car factory was a far cry from Nexus's high-tech, plush facility.

"Beautiful. Just beautiful," Tom said as Garrett led him down various corridors. "So, what exactly do you do every day?"

Garrett told him, introducing him to various members of the management team as they strolled along. After an hour, Garrett glanced at his watch. He still had business to attend to this afternoon but didn't want to be rude.

Tom seemed to take his cue. "I better go—I'm sure you have work to do. Thanks so much for the tour, Garrett. I can hardly wait to see your home and meet your wife and kids tomorrow night."

Garrett led him to the main lobby. "I wish I didn't have to work tonight, Dad, but some important stuff came up."

"No problem. Until tomorrow night then."

"I'll be in touch, Dad. I love you." They hugged, and Tom left through the front doors.

Around two thirty, Garrett headed over to Erin's office. He lingered at the door, unable to help overhearing Derek and Erin as they went over one of Derek's expense reports. It sounded like she was being fairly picky on some of his entries, and Derek sounded annoyed. Garrett was glad Erin was thorough when she had her "controller" hat on; that's how an accounting department should be.

Garrett waited until Derek departed before stepping in. "Erin, I need you to take off your controller hat for a minute and put on your human resources hat."

Erin tucked a red lock behind her ear. "That sounds interesting. Do you need to shut my door?"

Garrett shut the door for her and took a chair. "I wanted to talk to you about Carlton. I recently had a conversation with him and asked him some questions about his job activities. He got really defensive about it. I'm probably jumping to conclusions, but I've got some trust issues with him right now. I'm not sure if the feeling is valid, but I just can't shake it."

"The fact that he became defensive is disturbing, but that's not unusual for Carlton."

"I haven't told you about two odd incidents involving Carlton over the last couple of weeks. First, Kramer and I came out of the lab one day for lunch, and we found Carlton standing just outside the door. He didn't appear to be going anywhere, and he pretty much invited himself to lunch with us. The thought crossed my mind that he might have been trying to listen in on our conversation."

Erin nodded, a concerned look stealing into her eyes. "That's possible."

"Second, Kramer arrived to the lab early one morning and found Carlton working on his computer."

Erin arched an eyebrow. "Really."

"Yeah. And when Kramer asked Carlton what he was doing, he seemed rattled—like Kramer had caught him doing something wrong. So I'm starting to wonder what's going on."

"For good reason."

"I obtained information from our computer consulting company on how to look through his e-mail account. I wanted to let you know that I plan to take a peek and see if there's anything that might shed some light on his activities."

An unsettled look crept into her eyes.

"Erin, is something wrong?"

She hesitated. "Why didn't you bring this problem to

my attention earlier? That's why human resources is here—to handle employee problems like this. In fact, if you'd asked me first before calling our computer consulting company, I could have told you how to check his e-mail."

Garrett blushed, realizing he'd messed up. Sometimes he tried to fix things himself instead of going through the proper channels. "I'm sorry. I should have contacted you about this earlier. You know I have total trust in you and your ability to handle any problem. Sometimes I just get caught up in a situation and don't think about all my avenues for resolving it."

"It's really not that big of a deal. I just want to help you. You already have a lot on your plate. Probably too much." She cleared her throat. "Now, what are you looking for in his e-mails?"

"I think he might be trying to find confidential information about our research and development projects."

"For what reason?"

"I'm not sure. And really, it's just a hunch. I could be wrong."

"Searching through all his e-mails sounds like a lot of work. You want me to help you?"

"No, thanks. I think I should do this on my own. That way if I'm wrong, I'll be the only one wasting time."

He cringed. "Just the thought of looking at his e-mail makes me feel a little guilty, almost like I'm violating his privacy. But I need to find out if there's something going on that shouldn't be."

CHAPTER 10

Confrontation

Almost everyone had left the building for the day. Garrett thought the hallways and offices were quiet—eerily quiet—when he headed to the break room to brew another pot of coffee. When it was finished, he poured himself a fresh cup, stirred in some low-fat creamer, and headed back to his office, glancing at his watch.

It might be a long evening.

Good thing he'd called Margret and told her not to expect him for supper.

Back in his office, he froze and stared at his desk. His drawers hung opened, their contents moved. Papers, folders, and other contents were strewn across his desk and littered the floor. Half of his bookshelves had been emptied, and someone had scattered some of his books across the floor.

Fine hairs rose on the back of his neck as the blood drained from his face. He felt as if someone had punched him in the stomach.

Someone ransacked my office!—someone looking for something. But who? I wasn't gone that long. Where is the culprit now?

He reached for his phone and dialed security as his gaze strayed to his computer screen. His e-mail program was open, but he'd closed it not twenty minutes ago. Who had been going through his e-mail? And why?

A familiar voice picked up.

"Ted, this is Garrett. I'm glad you're still here."

"What's up?"

Garrett clasped his hands to stop their shaking. "My office. We may have an intruder in the building. Somebody emptied my drawers and threw all my books on the floor. There's a real mess here."

"I'll be right there."

Garrett retreated to the doorway, not wanting to touch anything. He searched the empty corridor; there was no one. Ted, a rail-thin man with a prominent Adam's apple, arrived minutes later, and Garrett explained that he'd gone to make a pot of coffee only to return to this.

"Does anything appear to be missing?"

"Not that I can tell, but I won't really know until I

put everything back. But if nothing is stolen, why would someone do this?"

"I don't know," Ted said, studying the scene. "Do you keep company secrets in here?"

"Maybe." Garrett rubbed the back of his neck, unwilling to admit to the whereabouts of any "company secrets," as Ted called them.

"From now on, keep your door locked at all times when you're not here. Even if you're just going to get some coffee."

"You're right. I shouldn't have left my door open. I guess I never thought something like this could happen."

"Well, you *are* the president of the company, and we do have competitors."

Ted said he'd do a survey of which employees had left the building and who were still working. He also agreed to check the rest of the facility for any signs of forced entry. Beyond that, he admitted, unless there was something stolen, there wasn't much more he could do.

"But don't we have security cameras?" Garrett asked.

"In the main lobby, yes, but not in all the hallways."

"Check the lobby footage and see if anyone entered the building today who doesn't belong."

"I'll get right on it, Garrett."

After putting his office back in order, Garrett sat at his desk and studied his e-mail program. There was no way of knowing what the intruder had seen. But why would someone do this? Had someone been looking for production information on B228? Who but he and Kramer knew anything about it? Could Carlton possibly be behind this?

He called Ted. "Do you know if Carlton Vance is still in the building?"

"No, he's gone."

"Okay, thanks, Ted."

Of course, that didn't mean anything. Carlton could have left immediately after ransacking his office.

Garrett decided not to put off what he'd been dreading any longer. He reviewed the instructions from the computer consulting company and pulled up Carlton's e-mail account. He started going through his e-mails by month, starting three months back and moving toward the present. The plentiful number of personal e-mails surprised him. He needed to check them all because they might contain the information he was looking for.

During the next hour, he went through two months of e-mails and found nothing. Had he overreacted?

At around eight thirty, he was tempted to skip the last month and go home to see his family, but he decided to keep plugging away. Soon, he came across a string of e-mails between Carlton and Health-fuze, Inc., Nexus's main competitor.

His heart raced as he clicked on the first e-mail. Feelings of anger and betrayal boiled up inside as he read:

Carlton,

We really look forward to having you join our team here at Health-fuze, Inc. soon. We would like to give you another month or two to gather any information you can from Nexus, Inc., especially in the area of research and development of new products.

Garrett leaned back in his chair, stunned. He began connecting all the dots from Carlton's activities over the last few weeks. Questions raced through his mind. Why would Carlton do this to Nexus? Was this proof that Carlton was the culprit who had gone through his drawers and e-mails, despite Ted's assurance that he had already left?

Garrett's habit was to extend unconditional trust to his employees, but had that been a mistake? Maybe he hadn't made people earn his trust often enough.

After fifteen minutes of thinking through the situation, he called Erin at home and updated her on what he'd found on Carlton. She was surprised. They discussed what they needed to do next.

Garrett already knew. Tomorrow would be a tough day.

As Garrett drove home that night, he wrestled with angry thoughts about the situation. At the same time, he felt sorry for Carlton. Everybody makes mistakes, but some mistakes seem worse than others, and Carlton's betrayal hurt. Why had Carlton chosen this path? They'd always treated him well at Nexus. Could Carlton be the one who searched his office? Had he been after B228?

That night Garrett struggled to sleep and grew restless, longing for the morning to come.

On Tuesday, he met with Erin in his office and discussed Carlton's termination. He was prepared to call Carlton in with her there as a witness from Human Resources. In the back of his mind, he hoped Carlton would be honest with him. Such a response would allow them to part on much better terms.

Erin called Carlton and asked him to meet her in Garrett's office. As the three of them sat in Garrett's office, tension filled the room. Garrett decided not to waste time.

"Carlton, it has come to my attention that you're planning to leave Nexus and work for Health-fuze, Inc., our main competitor. Is this true?"

Carlton's eyes widened in astonishment. "No, of course not. Where did you get that idea?"

Garrett struggled to hide his disappointment. He would have been happier if Carlton had admitted his guilt; then they could part on decent terms. Now he had no choice but to confront Carlton about the e-mail. If Carlton lied about it, he would have every valid and legal reason to fire him.

"Carlton, have you been in contact with Health-fuze, Inc., in the last three months, either by phone or e-mail, about working for them?"

Carlton's hands fidgeted. He gazed about the room as if looking for an escape, but he responded in a calm voice. "Garrett, I assure you that I have not been in contact with them via phone or e-mail—ever."

Garrett stared him down for a full five seconds. "I

have printouts of several e-mails that prove otherwise. Do you really want to see them?"

Carlton reddened, and sweat glistened on his forehead. "How did you get my e-mails?"

"It doesn't matter how," Garrett said, trying to keep his anger in check. "We need to terminate you. Pack up your things and leave right away."

Carlton's jaw tightened. The hands in his lap clenched. "I can promise you this. If you looked at my private e-mails to find dirt on me, you'd better get a good lawyer. I'm going to sue you for personal invasion."

Carlton got up and stormed out of the office. Erin rolled her eyes at Garrett and followed Carlton to make sure he left the property promptly and without incident.

For a few minutes Garrett sat in silence and reviewed the conversation. He folded his hands to keep them from shaking.

If only Carlton had been honest . . . the conversation would have ended much better. The threat of a lawsuit didn't bother him; the employee manual, which everyone on staff had signed, had Nexus covered. How Carlton had handled—or mishandled—the situation was so disappointing.

Garrett felt drained, both emotionally and physically.

Erin returned to Garrett's office with a grim look on her face. "I had security escort him to his car. He's gone." She paused. "Hey, you did the right thing."

"Thank you."

"Are you okay?"

"Yes, I'm fine. This sort of thing isn't fun for anyone, but it had to be done."

She nodded.

He sighed. "I'd like you to tell the staff we had to let Carlton go. If they ask why, just tell them he broke company policy. We should probably let the management team know the rest but tell them to keep the information to themselves. I'll talk to Kramer and let him know a little more because it involves his department."

"Do you think the ransacking of your office was Carlton's doing?" she asked.

"Maybe Carlton was trying to find information on my computer," He shrugged. "It would be hard to prove. I didn't bother asking him. I knew he'd just deny it. If it *was* him, he's gone now."

She rose and told him she hoped the rest of his day improved. Then she left.

Garrett glanced out the window. He had a sinking feeling that he hadn't heard the last of Carlton. He hoped

Carlton was honest about the situation when he shared the news with others. He could only control how he handled himself, not how Carlton handled himself.

He picked up the phone. When Kramer answered, he said, "Hey, it's me, Garrett. There's something you should know."

On Wednesday, Garrett sensed a different atmosphere when he arrived to his office. To his surprise, he sensed a more positive atmosphere from the secretaries and staff. He hadn't shared why he'd let Carlton go with everyone, though the management team knew. It seemed like everyone realized that whatever the reason, it was a good development.

Throughout the morning, he got the sense that even if employees didn't know the details, they respected his decisions and supported him. That feeling of support encouraged him. He had always sensed that his employees supported him, but this affirmation gave him a different feeling. And it was wonderful.

Ted called. "I reviewed yesterday's video footage of the main lobby. I didn't see anyone suspicious come in."

"Okay, thanks, Ted."

"So I can't explain who did it."

"That's all right. You did your best."

He hung up.

It was an inside job, right? Who else had been in his office lately?

Then he thought of Tom, his father, and the Nexus tour. Tom had been in his office. Briefly.

But what could his biological father have to do with any of this? He shrugged off the suspicion.

Garrett got right to work. He had an important board meeting that afternoon and prep work to finish. He'd invited prospective board members to visit today; that way, both Nexus and the prospective board members could see whether the union was a good fit. The importance of the meeting made him nervous. Add the Carlton termination and the fact that someone unknown had ransacked his office, and he felt more uptight than usual. He looked forward to the meal tonight with his family and his father. He could relax then.

The board meeting started at 1:00 p.m., and Garrett gave his normal updates on research and development, financials, marketing direction, and then Carlton. The board approved the stock options program for key employees. Garrett was enthusiastic about implementing this program; he hoped it would give key management staff a sense of ownership in the company, which in return would increase their desire to fulfill its mission.

Erin's call concluded the day on a sour note. "Carlton released a rant on social media."

Garrett wasn't surprised. "Was it specifically about Nexus or me?"

"He wasn't specific—he didn't name you or Nexus. But if you personally know him, you can figure out who he's talking about."

He decided to take the high road and not worry about Carlton. "Thanks for letting me know."

Just before he left, his phone rang. It was Ted from security. "I know this is going to sound strange, but there's something weird about your dad and the lobby footage."

"My father, Tom?" Garrett sat up straighter. "What are you saying?"

"Your father didn't leave through the front door."

"But of course he did. I walked him to the lobby myself and said goodbye. I saw him walk out."

"But he didn't leave. He went out the door, but then he came right back in. And what's weird is that he never left the building through the main lobby after that. I've checked and double-checked the footage."

"But why would he have gone out another way? He

didn't even know where the other exits were."

But you showed him the way around, didn't you?

"There could be a simple explanation," Ted said. "I'm sure it's nothing to worry about. After all, this is your father we're talking about."

Yes, that was true. But still, Garrett couldn't shake a new, unsettled feeling that dug in its claws. What if his dad had lingered in the building until Garrett stayed late and went to the break room to make coffee? Could his birth father have been the one who messed up his office and looked through his e-mail? But why would he do that?

Maybe he knew about B228 somehow.

But how?

No, it was too ridiculous. His father would never have done something like that.

Finally, Garrett pushed his suspicions aside and went home.

The meal with his father and his family was memorable and took his mind off his troubles.

But the Carlton termination and the mystery of the unknown intruder kept him awake again. At 1:00 a.m., he still couldn't sleep. He couldn't help wondering how far Carlton would go to get revenge. He could probably damage the company's good reputation if that's what he wanted to do.

Garrett told himself he was probably overreacting and tried to go to sleep.

But then his mind drifted to these new suspicions about his father. What did he really know about his dad? Maybe Tom wasn't really his father, after all. Could he be an imposter who was after the product secrets at Nexus?

No, that was crazy. Jerry had said he found Tom through a DNA match. Tom was flesh and blood.

Garrett rolled over and finally drifted off to sleep.

Chapter 11

Giving

Friday was an unusual day for Nexus. When Garrett appeared for breakfast dressed in work jeans and a t-shirt, Margret did a double take. "What's up? Aren't you going to work today?"

"It's that work day I told you about—John's idea, though Erin's done a lot of the planning. The employees have been invited to help a local nonprofit build a house for a needy family."

"So Nexus is shutting down for the day?"

"Yep, the whole place."

"I think that's great to be giving back to the community."

"Construction work is way out of my comfort zone, as you know, but it's important to be part of the team."

She patted his back and poured his coffee. "This'll be good for you. Get your mind off Carlton."

And my father. He hadn't told her about his new suspicions regarding Tom, though he knew they were probably groundless.

The building project was located in nearby Charlotte, in a rough part of town. Garrett made sure to lock his car doors. The fact that about twenty-five employees had already arrived lifted his spirits.

Right away, he could tell John was in his element. He was organizing supplies, people, and duties. It was obvious he wanted to get some work done and make a difference for the people in this neighborhood.

Garrett greeted him, and John put him to work organizing tools and supplies.

Erin and Kari had ridden together and pulled up in a flashy sports car, definitely *not* dressed for construction work.

"Hey, you made it." John grinned. He glanced at their feet. "Well, at least you didn't wear high heels."

"Is there anything we can do?" Erin asked.

"In those clothes?" he shook his head. "Not much."

"We could wash windows," Kari suggested.

"Go to it."

By 9:00 a.m. the project was in full swing. When Garrett glanced up, he noticed they had a visitor. A homeless man with a long, scraggly beard and filthy clothes watched from the nearby sidewalk while the Nexus team worked.

The man stepped closer, and Derek approached him. Garrett assumed Derek was making chitchat in an attempt to befriend the man, but moments later a look of anger flashed across Derek's face. Then Derek chased the homeless man off the site with a stick.

Garrett put down his hammer and stared at Derek with an undisguised mix of anger and disbelief. How could Derek treat a homeless man that way? When Derek glanced his direction, Garrett shot him a look of disapproval. There couldn't be any confusion that Garrett was displeased with how Derek had handled the situation.

The mood lightened when they started interior work. Kramer, clad in overalls and a sweat-soaked shirt, asked Garrett to help him nail down some floorboards.

"Garrett, do you know how to use a nail gun?" Kramer asked.

Garrett didn't want to appear clueless. Besides, how hard could it be? "Sure. No problem."

"I heard that somebody messed up your office the

other night. Does Ted have any idea who did it?"

"Nope. Not yet. He's still looking into it."

Kramer lowered his voice so they wouldn't be overheard. "Do you think it could have something to do with a certain project and Carlton?"

"Maybe. Have you checked your flash drive backups lately?"

"Yeah. Everything's fine."

As they nailed down the flooring, Garrett realized this work could be really rewarding and fun. He was starting to get comfortable with the gun when he made a big mistake. As he shot the final nail for the current floorboard, he accidentally nailed his shoe to the floor. Embarrassed, he tried to pull the nail out, but it wouldn't budge. Then he tried to take off his shoe, but the nail was between two toes, and the shoe was too tight to get off.

"Uh, Kramer," Garrett said in an embarrassed voice. "I've got a little problem over here."

Kramer surveyed the situation. At first, he tried to keep a straight face, but then he couldn't stop laughing. He wasted no time in calling the others over.

"Hey, John. Come see. The boss nailed himself to the floor!"

The news spread throughout the construction site. Garrett could only stand there, blushing.

Derek, who was pouring cement out front, ran in to see. "Hey, did someone get a picture of this yet?"

Five minutes later, the whole thing was described in a post on a popular social media outlet. Garrett decided to be a good sport and smiled for the camera while pointing at his nailed-down shoe.

John freed Garrett and gave him a broom. "There. I think you better stick to equipment that's a little . . . uh . . . safer." They chuckled together, and Garrett gave him an affectionate slap on the back.

When they took a break for lunch, everybody sat down to enjoy sub sandwiches and a choice of bottled water or a Nexus health drink, compliments of Nexus, Inc. Like many other lunchtimes, everybody started pulling out smartphones to check e-mails, texts, and the Internet. Garrett glanced toward Derek and almost dropped his roast beef sub.

Derek had invited the homeless man to eat with him. Garrett's heart melted at the sight of Derek sharing half of his sub with the same man he'd driven off the property only a few hours ago. Seeing Derek's generous spirit to someone so unlovely yet needy made the whole work project seem worth it.

As lunch drew to a close, Erin pulled Garrett aside. "I'm afraid looks can be deceiving," she said.

"What do you mean?"

"I've gotten some complaints. Not all employees are thrilled about the work project."

Garrett frowned. "I don't understand."

The breeze tousled her red hair. "We shut the plant down, but some employees really wanted to work. They say they need the hours and the money."

Garrett shook his head in frustration. "I was trying to do a good thing with this project."

"And it *is* a good thing."

"But I guess I didn't think through how it might affect some of our hourly employees."

She nodded. "This gives them one less workday this week."

"Let's deal with this on Monday. They might be able to pick up a few extra hours next week."

As he walked away, he shook his head.

I try so hard to make good decisions everyone will support, but it's impossible.

To make matters worse, Garrett later had an unsettling experience at the barber shop, where he dropped by for his customary haircut. Fred, a portly man with a round face, had cut his hair for years and was usually fun to talk to.

"Some of my customers told me about employee problems you must be having over at Nexus," Fred said. "Are you in legal trouble?"

He must have heard about Carlton.

Garrett tried to hide his frustration. "Fred, living in a smaller town like Monroe can sometimes lend itself to rumors. You know that, right?"

He left it at that.

CHAPTER 12

Sacrifice

"Okay, Kari. Go ahead." Garrett said, resting his folded hands on the conference table. "What do you have to report?"

It was their regular Monday morning meeting. A week had passed since Carlton's termination, and Garrett was hoping for good news.

Kari from Customer Relations was going over quality complaints. "I'm afraid they're on the rise."

The team members shook their heads or frowned. Garrett asked how they could improve in this area, and several gave suggestions.

"As you know," he said, "customer feedback is very important. I've tried to personally reply to all complaints myself. That way, I'm in touch with the problems.

Besides"—he shrugged—"I think it means more to cus-tomers when the president of the company takes time to personally respond to their complaints."

Next, John gave a report on a new plan to increase the efficiency of the arthritis cream line. This was the second plan because the first plan, the one John had in-sisted on but that Garrett hadn't liked, had failed. Garrett could have told them this second plan was really *his* plan, but he wasn't interested in getting credit. He wanted to build John up, not make him look bad.

During the last ten minutes, Garrett handed each member a book he wanted the team to read. "I think you'll learn a lot from this book," he said. "I know I did."

"Oh, that's right," Derek said, examining the cover of the book with a boyish grin. "Each year you give us a new book to read, don't you?"

"That's right, and we're going to be taking some time during the next few management team meetings to dis-cuss it."

He knew some of them struggled to get excited about this project, but usually in the end they were happy they'd read the book.

After the meeting, Garrett asked Derek to meet him

in his office to go over some sales items. They had just sat down and gotten started when the receptionist called and asked Garrett to come to the lobby and sign for some certified mail addressed to him.

Garrett got up. "Don't go anywhere. I'll be right back."

While Derek waited, his gaze drifted to Garrett's computer and the e-mail open on his screen. He knew he shouldn't be a snoop, but what would a quick glance hurt? It was probably just an e-mail from his wife about dinner plans.

He was wrong:

> Garrett,
>
> I've hired an attorney, and you'll be hearing from him very soon.
> YOU ARE GOING TO WISH YOU HAD NEVER READ MY E-MAIL!!!
>
> Carlton

Derek sank back into his chair, mind whirling. He, of course, knew about Carlton's termination and the fact that he'd been spying for a competitor—information revealed from his e-mails. Though the employee policy manual had Nexus covered in a legal sense, the e-mail was still threatening and a little scary.

Carlton wasn't happy about his termination. Not at all. It was amazing how well Garrett handled himself around others with stuff like this hanging over his head.

Derek repositioned his chair so the computer screen was more difficult to see; he didn't want Garrett to know he'd seen the e-mail.

Moments later, Garrett reentered the room and resumed his seat, dropping an envelope on his desk. "Sorry about that."

"Everything okay, Garrett?"

Garrett waved away his concern. "Oh sure. Everything's fine. I just had to sign for this certified letter. No biggie."

After Derek returned to his office, he paced back and forth in front of his desk, unable to get the threatening e-mail out of his head. The fact that Garrett had to deal with threats like that angered him.

He reached for his phone. "Hey, John. Do you mind dropping by for a few minutes?"

Thirty seconds later, John appeared. "Hey, what's up?"

After John closed the door, Derek told him what he'd seen. "We need to go out of our way to encourage Garrett," John said.

Derek nodded. "Let's plan on it. I think he needs our support now more than ever."

The next day at 11:55 a.m., just when Garrett was getting ready to leave for lunch, his phone rang. It was John.

"Hey, we've got a big problem out here. I need your help."

Garrett glanced at his watch. "Right now? It's almost lunchtime."

"Sorry. You might have to miss lunch today. This is a *big* problem."

"Be right there." Garrett hung up and sighed. What could be so serious? His mind plowed through all sorts of gut-wrenching scenarios, and he broke into a cold sweat.

He strode to the warehouse and pushed his way through the doors.

"Happy birthday!"

He jumped back, surrounded by the smiling faces of so many people he knew and loved. "What's this? My birthday isn't until Saturday!"

"We don't work on Saturday," Erin said, tossing a small handful of confetti, "so we're celebrating today."

Garrett's ears burned. He hated being the center of attention. He followed his nose and found two tables heaped with Mexican food, his favorite.

"Wow, I'm touched by your thoughtfulness!" he said, amid congratulations and plenty of backslapping.

The food was delicious, and the meal together provided a great opportunity for the team to bond. It wasn't very often that all employees enjoyed a meal together in the same place at the same time. Garrett took the opportunity to move around the room and chat with as many employees as he could, especially the ones he rarely saw.

But he couldn't help wondering as he spoke to each one, *Is this the guy who ransacked my office?*

By 1:00 p.m. the party was over, and Garrett was in a meeting with Kari and Derek.

"We've got a new idea for marketing our products." Derek's voice reverberated with excitement.

"We think you'll really like it," Kari said.

Garrett was thrilled that Derek and Kari had worked together on this idea. "Okay. Show me what you've got."

With plenty of eye-popping visuals and a rehearsed script, they pitched the idea of Nexus signing on several celebrity athletes to endorse their products. Garrett scratched his chin, realizing that he'd never thought of this opportunity before.

"So what do you think?" Kari asked when they were finished.

Garrett took a moment to choose his words carefully. "I'm not against the idea—truly I'm not."

"But?" Derek said. Hope still shone in his eyes.

"I have two concerns: cost and vulnerability."

Kari said, "Well then, let's discuss those, one at a time."

"It would cost a bundle to get product endorsements from the big-name athletes you recommend."

"I think we can clearly show that we'd make more money than we'd spend," Derek said. "We have studies to back up that claim."

"Okay," Garrett said. "But what about vulnerability? Have you thought that through?"

They stared at him as if he'd grown antlers.

Garrett spread his hands. "Even if you signed on someone with an excellent reputation now, what if that athlete was later found guilty of a terrible scandal? Can you imagine the negative impact that endorsement would have on our product line?"

They hung their heads. They clearly hadn't explored

this issue as thoroughly as they should have.

"Remember, these athletes are always in the lime-light," Garrett said. "Their behavior is closely scrutinized. While I'm not against the idea, we have to remember that this would be a big gamble. And I've never been much of a gambler, especially when it comes to big dollars and this company's reputation."

They remained silent. Garrett hated to see them look so downcast.

"Look," he said. "This has been a great meeting, and your presentation was excellent. Good job! I'm not prepared to say no just yet."

They glanced up, smiles on their faces.

"Now hold on! I just want time to give your idea more consideration, and I'll get back to you. How does that sound?"

After lunch, Garrett's phone rang. It was his dad.

"Hey, Garrett. I got your message and wanted to call you back."

"Hey, Dad. I just wanted to say hi and see how you're doing."

"Oh, I'm just fine. That sure was nice of you to give me the tour of Nexus. I had a great time. And then meeting your family was priceless."

"They were glad to meet you too. Say, Dad, there's something I wanted to ask you."

"And what's that?"

Garrett hesitated. He didn't want to accuse his dad of anything without evidence. "When I gave you the tour of Nexus the other day, did you come back into the building after we said goodbye?"

"Yeah, I did. I noticed a full pot of coffee in the lobby on my way out." He chuckled. "Hope you don't mind. I went back and filled a tall cup for the road. I had a long drive ahead of me—remember, I wanted to check out that auto museum you recommended—and I didn't want to fall asleep at the wheel."

Oh, that was it. Garrett relaxed. "But then how did you leave the building?"

A moment of silence. "Garrett, why are you asking me all these questions?"

"We might have had an intruder in the building that day, and security is just double-checking how everyone entered and left the building."

"Oh, I see. Well, after I got my coffee, one of your pretty receptionists in the lobby chatted with me and realized I was your dad. She saw my coffee and said there was much better coffee near the administrative offices. So she showed me the nicer break room near your office that has the cool coffee machine and then left me there. But after I filled my cup, I somehow got turned around and lost my way."

Garrett chuckled, relieved. "So how did you find your way out?"

"I wandered around until I ended up in the production warehouse. One of the big bay doors opened for a shipment, and I walked right out through there."

"I'm glad you got out okay, Dad. Thanks for letting me know."

Around two thirty, Garrett was working alone in his office, developing future goals for the next management meeting. The fire alarm sounded suddenly, making him jump. He sighed, shook his head, and rose from his chair. The fire alarm had gone off a few times before, so he didn't take it seriously. They had always been false alarms.

Garrett stepped out of his office and spoke with his secretaries. They hadn't sensed any traces of smoke or fire.

He called John in production to see if he knew anything.

No answer.

Meanwhile, the blaring alarm made his ears ache.

The staff routinely evacuated the building in these situations, but he usually held off until he had more information.

The alarm continued to blare, and his secretaries pressed their hands over their ears. He advised them to go ahead and evacuate.

He headed down the hall to investigate. When he reached the fire alarm's system information panel near the maintenance department, he paused. He peered down the empty corridor. Where was everybody?

Frowning, he studied the information panel, and his pulse quickened. According to the display, a problem in the production area had triggered the alarm. Was John battling flames? Was that why he hadn't answered the phone?

Then, the first traces of smoke curled into the hall. The smell was strong.

The door beside him sprang open. At least a dozen employees rushed out.

Is this really happening?

Garrett raised his arms and hushed their excited voices. He told them to go outdoors and wait at the designated meeting point. Then he raced to the production area to find John. At the end of the large production room, smoke curled and grew out from the cracks around a closed door that led to an adjacent hall. Garrett stopped in his tracks.

Flames leaped up around the door. John wielded a fire extinguisher, and two coworkers battled the flames by beating them with floor mats. Yet, the fire consumed the door and spread to the wall, clearly beyond their control. The production area would soon be engulfed in flames.

Garrett flew into action, arriving at John's side in mere seconds. The fire's searing heat made sweat erupt from Garrett's pores. The smoke burned his throat and made him cough.

Garrett yelled to John's crew over the roaring fire and told them to get out. As the pair raced toward a safe exit, Garrett gripped John's shoulder and choked out, "What happened?"

John shook the extinguisher, desperately trying to get more spray for the fire, his bald head shiny with sweat. Soot blackened his face and clothes. "I don't know! I think the mixer overheated and caught fire!"

"Did you call the fire department?"

John nodded and lowered the empty extinguisher. "Yes, they're on their way."

Garrett took a quick look around the smoky room to ensure no other employees were in harm's way. "We need to get out of here!"

They turned and ran for the exit.

"I'm so sorry," John choked out. "This is my fault—I should have caught the fire earlier."

"John, stop. It doesn't matter. We just need to get out."

They found an exit at the end of another hall. Once outside the building, Garrett led a roll call with all managers and their employees. His stomach churned. "Where's Kramer? Anybody seen him?"

One of the research and development guys ran up. "He told us to evacuate and said he'd be right behind us. He just needed to retrieve some important information."

"You mean—he's still in there?" Smoke drifted out of the windows and doors now. If the smoke was that thick, Kramer could be in serious danger—or even dead.

Garrett didn't hear any fire truck sirens yet. He couldn't wait for help, not when Kramer's life was in danger. He sprinted toward the door closest to research and development and headed into the smoke.

The B228 project. That's why Kramer had gone back—Garrett was sure of it. If he didn't retrieve those flash drives from his file cabinet, the product data would go up in smoke. They would lose all their research.

Garrett headed down the hall and took a right toward

the lab. He untucked his shirt and breathed through his shirttail to screen the smoke. Then he got lower to the floor where the smoke wasn't as bad. The smoke burned his lungs and stung his eyes. Tears fell down his cheeks.

"Kramer!" he yelled. "Kramer?"

No answer.

The room was so hot his skin burned. His heart raced.

"Kramer!"

Then a voice to his right. "Over here!"

Garrett closed his eyes to keep the smoke from stinging them and followed the hot wall with his scorched hands toward the lab offices. The whole place was like an oven.

He almost walked into Kramer. He lay in the corner, curled up in a ball.

Garrett knelt beside him and placed a hand on Kramer's sweat-drenched hair. "Kramer, what are you doing? We need to get out of here."

Panic rang in Kramer's voice. "I can't—I can't find my way out."

"I know the way. Did you get it? The plans for B228?"

"Yes." Kramer peered up at Garrett with eyes bloodshot from smoke irritation. "The flash drives are in my pockets. I wouldn't let him have them."

Garrett gripped his shoulders. "Who?"

"Tim, that new guy in maintenance. He told me he'd set the place on fire if I didn't give him the plans for B228. When I didn't do what he wanted, he began lighting fires."

The fire had been started deliberately. Garrett could hardly believe it. How did the new guy know about B228? "Where is he now?"

"I don't know. He had a gas tank, and it looked like he was heading to other parts of the building."

"That doesn't matter now. We need to get out of here. Follow me!"

"I can't get up," Kramer said. "I don't have any strength." He started coughing and couldn't stop.

Garrett stripped off his shirt until he was wearing only his T-shirt. He wrapped the shirt around Kramer's head. "This'll help you breathe better. Put your arm around my neck." Kramer managed to do that. "Okay, good," Garrett encouraged him. "Now let's go!"

Garrett lifted Kramer to his feet and led him around the corner and down the long hall toward the exit. As Garrett peered through the smoke, he realized they were in big trouble. Part of the burning ceiling had begun to fall in; if they didn't hurry, it would soon block the exit.

Visibility was next to nothing now, and Garrett couldn't take a breath without coughing. His lungs hurt so badly.

He pushed Kramer ahead of him to ensure he'd get out first. Twelve feet from the exit door, relief rushed through him. Yes, they were going to make it!

A loud cracking sound overhead froze Garrett in his tracks. As he looked up, a huge piece of the ceiling came crashing down.

With Garrett's shirt pressed to his face, Kramer rose on weak legs and searched the smoky debris with burning eyes.

"Garrett!" he shouted. "Garrett, where are you?" Kramer couldn't leave without him.

"Garrett?"

No answer.

He felt along the burning wall with his seared hands and backtracked. When he found Garrett lying on the floor, his heart sank. A large section of the ceiling framework had knocked Garrett to the floor, pinning him down. Garrett's face twisted in pain as he pushed against the debris with his hands and tried to pull his legs free.

Kramer tried to lift the hot debris off Garrett's legs, but

it was no use. It was too heavy. Besides, he couldn't stop coughing, and what little strength he had was almost spent.

"Go, Kramer!" Garrett shouted. "Get out!"

Tears stung Kramer's burning eyes. "No! I'm not leaving without you!"

"The fire fighters can help. Go! They'll be able to help me. Now hurry!"

With one anguished glance at his boss, Kramer ran. He burst through the exit door, instantly awash in fresh air. He stumbled toward a crowd of employees standing and watching helplessly as the building burned. Someone shouted his name.

He stumbled to his knees. Out of breath. Out of strength. Employees surrounded him.

"Kramer, where's Garrett?" It was John. His voice shook with panic. "Did you see him in there?"

Kramer tried to respond but succumbed to a fit of coughing. He pointed at the exit door.

A fireman wielding an axe raced past him, opened the smoking door, and disappeared inside. A cloud of smoke poured out. Two more firemen ran after their comrade and headed inside too.

Still on the ground, Kramer took slow, deep gasps of air, his heart pounding as if it might burst. He could breathe more easily now, but he had no strength, not even to stand. A Latino woman in an EMT uniform ran toward him with a gurney and helped him onto it. She pressed an oxygen mask to his face.

He took great gulps of air. Stared at the exit door.

What was taking so long? Where were the firemen with Garrett? He couldn't be far from the door.

Fire leaped from the roof, bursting up at least ten feet into the air. He could only imagine the fire inside. How could Garrett still be in there and survive the heat and smoke?

Another EMT arrived and checked his vitals. The two EMTs began rolling him toward an ambulance when the exit door burst open. Three firemen emerged from the blinding cloud of smoke. One carried Garrett over his shoulder.

"Wait!" Kramer croaked.

The EMTs stopped the gurney and abandoned Kramer to run back and assist the firemen.

Garrett hung limply over the fireman's shoulder. He appeared to be unconscious. The EMTs lowered him to another gurney and began working on him.

Too much smoke. Too much heat.

Kramer was afraid to ask, but he had to know. He

pulled off the oxygen mask.

"How is he?" he called hoarsely. "Somebody please tell me. Is he okay?"

The firemen didn't answer. The EMTs didn't say anything either; they just kept working on Garrett. Kramer couldn't see past their backs. What were they doing to him?

One of the EMTs returned and pushed him toward an ambulance, face grim.

"Is my friend going to be okay?" Kramer asked.

"It doesn't look good, but he might still pull through."

★ ★ ★

John peered through the rear window of the ambulance, trying to see inside. He smeared tears away, whether from smoke or grief, he couldn't say. He couldn't stop pacing. Adrenaline had kicked in, and he needed a way to use it.

At least he could tell they were working on Garrett. That was a good sign, right?

The ambulance pulled away, lights flashing. John stared at it in a daze.

Erin patted his back. "Word is they're taking him to Memorial." She sounded like she had a cold, but he knew she'd been crying.

He headed back to the mob of confused and grief-stricken employees. They milled around as if unsure what to do with themselves, one name on their lips: Garrett. Most looked confused and distraught. Many were crying. They seemed as out of control as the fire that continued to consume the roof and glow from glassless windows.

Fire trucks had lined up alongside the brick building, and firemen were spraying the fire with their hoses. John was no expert, but it looked to him like the building was a total loss.

He raised his arms and called out to try to create some sense of order. His colleagues began gathering around him in subdued silence, their faces anxious. He told them the ambulances were headed to Memorial Hospital.

"I'm sure the management team should head over there, but there probably isn't room for all of you." He cleared his throat. "Julissa, raise your hand. Everybody see Julissa? All right, make sure she has your phone number. I'll send you text updates. I'm sorry, but I don't know any more than you do. I'll send you news as soon as I have something I can share. There's nothing more you can do here. Go home and wait for word. I'll be in touch."

The crowd began to disperse, and the ashen-faced secretary was mobbed.

John stepped aside and dialed Margret's number. She answered after the second ring.

"Margret, this is John at Nexus."

"Yes?"

"I'm afraid there's been a fire."

"Oh no!"

"Garrett's been taken to Memorial Hospital. You need to get there as soon as possible."

Her voice rose in panic. "What happened? Did he get burned?"

"I don't know, but he's hurt." The reality of Garrett's possible injuries slammed into him, and his throat tightened. He could barely talk. "Just get there as quickly as you can."

CHAPTER 13

Adversity

While the ambulance sped toward the hospital, Sandra, a nurse in the hospital's emergency room, called the ambulance, requesting vital information about their patient.

After getting the usual details, she asked, "Do you have the identity of the patient?"

"Garrett Thompson," the EMT said.

"Garrett Thompson?" She was unable to keep the surprise out of her voice. "You mean, *the* Garrett Thompson of Nexus, Inc.?"

"Yes."

"Okay. Thank you." She hung up.

Immediately the room quieted as nurses and ER doctors stopped what they were doing and turned to stare at her. Of course, she didn't need to tell them who Garrett Thompson was. Many of them, including her, had been his coworkers during the time he spent there as a doctor. She knew the kind of person Garrett was and what he represented in their community.

Somberness filled the room, along with a quiet determination. She turned to her colleagues and swallowed hard. "All right, you heard who's on his way," she said as tears started to pool in her eyes. "We need to give Garrett our best work ever."

Nods from everyone in the room.

"Let's go."

Minutes later, paramedics wheeled Garrett into the emergency room. He looked bad. Sandra followed the gurney and spoke to the EMTs in hushed tones, assessing his condition. One of the doctors was worried about the lack of oxygen and the condition of his lungs. Everyone got busy and went to work.

Erin was sitting in the hospital lobby with Derek, her hands cold, when Margret arrived, her face streaked with tears.

Erin rose and greeted her with a hug. "Mrs. Thompson, he's in a coma, but he's still alive."

Margret visibly relaxed, but tears spilled from her eyes. "Where is he? Can I see him?"

"He's in the emergency room right now. I'm sorry. Nobody can see him."

"Who can I talk to?"

"The doctor said he'd meet us here and give us a report when he has one."

The sliding doors opened behind Margret. In walked John with Jasmine and Carter, who'd been let out of school early because of the accident. John had given them a ride. They hugged their mother, and everyone cried.

Margret turned to Erin. "Could someone please tell me what happened?"

Erin put an arm round her shoulders. "Margret, let's take a walk. I'll tell you everything I know."

For the next ten minutes, Erin explained the day's events. Margret couldn't control her sobbing until Erin found a restroom, where Margret could collect herself. Margret gave Erin the phone numbers of her parents and Garrett's parents, so Erin could contact them. She also gave her Tom's phone number in Detroit.

"Tom?" Erin asked.

"Garrett's biological father. He'll be so upset when he hears about this."

When they returned to the waiting room, Erin stared, overwhelmed by the sight. The room was crammed with more than thirty people, mostly Nexus employees. But there were some faces she didn't know. News of the fire had traveled fast, and many had come to pay their respects and wait for word.

"How could all these people care so much?" Margret said, more to herself than to Erin.

Since so many people had arrived, the medical staff moved Margret and her immediate family to a smaller waiting room and didn't let anyone in except family and the Nexus management team.

The door opened, and in walked Kramer. His clothes were sooty, and he looked pale, but he said he was going to be fine. He'd been transferred from the Nexus plant to the hospital by ambulance and was still under hospital care. The staff had allowed him to make a brief visit to Margret and the team, but he needed to return to his room soon for more tests.

His presence lifted the spirits in the room. Kramer was all right. Surely Garrett would be all right too.

He squeezed Margret's hand. "Don't worry. Garrett's a fighter, and he'll make it through this."

"But what was he doing in that burning building?"

Margret asked. "That's what I don't understand."

Kramer swallowed hard, and his eyes watered. "He came after me. I went back for some important product information and got lost in the smoke. Margret, your husband saved my life today. I'm sure he's going to be fine."

She gripped his arm. "But the fire. How did it start?"

"Tim, a new hire. He was acting like a madman and started the fire. I already talked to the police. They're trying to find him now."

Erin stared at him. John had told her that he thought it was an accident in the production area. "What?"

"He demanded confidential information about some of our new products—said he'd burn the place down if I didn't give him what I had. I was sure he was bluffing. When I refused, he started the fire. I know that—"

A hush interrupted him.

The doctor appeared in the doorway, a heavy man with a bull neck. When everyone quieted, he said, "I just want you to know they're working on Garrett right now, and I hope to have an update within the hour."

Margret crossed the room, introduced herself as Garrett's wife, and gripped his hands. "Tell me the truth.

How is he?"

"I won't mislead you. It's very serious. He's in critical condition, but he's still alive."

A sense of hope and caution swept through the room.

After the doctor left, Kramer slipped out to return to his room for more treatment. Erin offered to get drinks for Margret, her family, and members of the management team. John offered to help, and Derek stayed behind with Margret.

Erin and John took the elevator to the main lobby to find the vending machines. As she turned the corner, she couldn't believe her eyes.

The group of more than thirty had mushroomed to at least seventy-five. She recognized a lot of Nexus employees as well as other townspeople.

The room quieted as John gave them the doctor's report. "I'm sorry. That's all I know. I wish I knew more."

As they headed toward the vending machines in the corner, she froze and grabbed John's arm. Carlton sat on a chair in the corner by himself, head down, face in his hands.

"What are you doing here?" John's voice trembled with rage. "You're responsible for this fire, aren't you!"

Maybe so, Erin thought. *Maybe Carlton put Tim up to it.*

When Carlton lifted his head, Erin stared in surprise. The man with the model good looks appeared to be a broken man; his nose was red, his face streaked with tears. He struggled to get his words out. "No, I had nothing to do with the fire—you have to believe me." He sighed. "I was wrong, guys. I was very wrong. I treated Garrett just terrible. I only wanted to be close to him. Please . . . please let me stay. I'm so sorry."

John and Erin exchanged wary glances. Erin didn't know whether to trust him. The police would determine who was responsible. Until then, she'd have to give him the benefit of the doubt.

They turned to leave just as the fire chief walked in with an update. The fire was out, and portions of the building had been destroyed. But, thankfully, the building wasn't a total loss.

"Dad, how are you doing?"

Erin's head jerked to the right as John inhaled sharply. "Son, what are you doing here?" he said.

Erin remembered that Sam, John's son, had recently suffered a drug overdose. If so, he looked pretty good for just being in the hospital.

Sam looked into his father's eyes and put a hand on his

shoulder. "Dad, I'm here for you and Garrett. You guys did the same for me when I was in the hospital."

John hugged his son. "Dad, I hope Garrett makes it," Sam said into his shoulder. "I know he's important to you."

They pulled apart, and John looked into his son's eyes. "Sam, thanks so much for coming. It really means a lot to me. We need to get back to Margret, but I'll keep you posted."

"Okay, Dad." Sam waved as they walked away.

Back in the waiting room with Margret, Erin felt the tension in the room. Few people were talking now. It was close to 4:00 p.m., and everyone was waiting for another report from the doctor. Finally, almost a half hour later, a different doctor entered the room.

"Oh, it's Dr. Barron," Margret told Erin. "He's a family friend. Maybe he has some news." She crossed the room to greet him. Erin followed, unsure if he was the bearer of good news or bad. His face said nothing.

He gestured to two chairs, and he and Margret sat down. He took her hands in his and peered into her eyes.

"Doc, tell me. How is Garrett?" Margret's voice shook.

Only then did his eyes fill with tears. "Margret, it's over. We couldn't save him. I'm so very sorry."

Silence embraced the room. Erin took a deep, shuttering breath. She looked at the doctor to ensure they'd heard him correctly. He was crying, which doctors don't usually do, but he too had lost a friend.

Erin looked around the room, took in the deathly silence. Everyone seemed to be in shock. Just two hours ago, Garrett had been working in his office. Now life had changed for all of them.

"No!" The anguished cry tore from Margret's lips. She began to sob uncontrollably. Dr. Barron caught her as she went to crumple to the floor, but she pulled away and curled up into the fetal position.

Erin dropped to her knees and rubbed Margret's back, trying to do something to comfort her. But there was little anyone could do to make this news any easier. Margret had just lost her best friend, the kids had lost their father, and the Nexus team had lost their inspirational leader.

Erin bit her lip as tears welled up in her eyes and spilled down her cheeks. Garrett was needed; all of them had depended on him for something. Nothing seemed right about this moment. For most of them, Garrett was simply the best person they'd ever known

And now he was gone.

In their grief, no one made phone calls or sent text messages. Dr. Barron spent time with the group as they mourned their loss. The anguish Erin sensed in the room was unlike anything she'd experienced before.

Finally, Margret lay spent. Erin gently pulled at her, and she rose to her chair and rubbed her hands over her face. It was too late to say goodbye to her beloved husband, but she asked the doctor if she could see him. He nodded and led her out of the room.

In a hushed voice, John told Erin he wanted to break the news to Kramer and left, shoulders drooping. While Kari stayed behind with Margret's kids, Erin's feet carried her to the waiting room to break the news she'd never dreamed of sharing.

She sucked in a calming breath and let it out slowly. Margret, the kids, and the Nexus team would never be the same again. How could they recover from such a dreadful blow?

CHAPTER 14

Honor

Four days after the worst day of her life, Margret found herself sitting in the front row of their home church, just a block from their house. As she looked down the pew at her kids, she wondered how Garrett's death would affect Carter and Jasmine. They were old enough to understand what had happened, but maybe they were too young to fully grasp its meaning.

As she looked around at the people filling the auditorium for the funeral, she felt overwhelmed. The church was simply too small for all those who wanted to attend. Several friends had asked if Margret could move the service to a bigger church, but she knew Garrett would have wanted the service here, where he worshiped every Sunday morning.

And now we can worship here with him one last time.

The Nexus management team sat close behind the Thompson family. With sweaty palms, Kramer folded and unfolded the typed eulogy Margret had asked him to give. Though he was out of the hospital, he felt far from recovered. He sighed and wondered what people expected. Many thought of him as a biotechnologist. He certainly was no public speaker.

As he nervously waited to speak, he couldn't help but reflect on his shortcomings, his divorce, and his lack of effort to keep close to his family. Garrett had always tried to help other people. In fact, of all people in this world, he had trusted Garrett most, and now the man he'd trusted was gone. He'd never expressed this trust to him, but a small voice inside him whispered that Garrett probably realized it anyway.

Someone squeezed his shoulder. He turned.

"It's time for your eulogy," Erin whispered.

As he stood in front of the packed room, Kramer didn't feel worthy of this honor. To speak on behalf of Garrett Thompson was more than he deserved. Though he stumbled around a bit, people later told him he did an excellent job. One thing he knew for sure: there wasn't a dry eye in the room. As he drew to a close, emotion clogged his throat.

"Garrett saved my life when I was caught in that fire. He sacrificed his life for mine." He took a deep breath and tried to hold his emotions back. "A greater gift can no man ask for. He challenged us all to be better people. I'll personally never, *never* let him down."

Kramer folded the paper and returned to the pew, collapsing wearily in his seat. Then a funny thing happened. When the pastor opened up the service for a sharing time, person after person stood up and gave similar teary accounts.

Garrett had loved and cared for each person in his life as if he or she was the most important person to him. Just when Kramer felt that Garrett had loved him the most, someone else stood up and said he or she felt the same way.

Kramer nodded to himself. *Yeah, that's what made Garrett Thompson so special. That's what made him different from a lot of people. He truly cared.*

After the funeral was over, Kramer joined John and Derek as they chatted with the police chief. The police had arrested Tim, the man responsible for the fire. He claimed that he'd been hired by one of the major pharmaceutical companies to either steal Nexus's classified research or sabotage it. Perhaps he had even been the one who ransacked Garrett's office, looking for information. The police would need to finish their investigation to determine the validity of his story.

Now Tim would face murder charges for the death of Garrett Thompson. It would be an open-and-shut case.

Erin strolled over and joined them. After the police chief left, she said, "Hey, before all of you leave, I wanted to touch base about Nexus. The board of directors has agreed to rent some office space for now—I'm sure you've heard."

They nodded.

"Margret would like all of us to meet in a couple of weeks," she said. "She has something she wants to say, and we need to do some planning to keep the business going during this time of transition." They all agreed.

As Kramer left the funeral, he sensed that, in some strange way, none of them wanted to leave. A different life awaited them, one without Garrett, and he wasn't sure what kind of life that would be.

CHAPTER 15

Dedication

Derek peered out the window of his rented office, again feeling like something was missing. He knew what was gone. It was Garrett. Had two weeks really gone by since Nexus lost its leader and his father figure?

His phone rang. It was Clyde, one of their vendors.

"How are things going there?" he asked. "I read all about your tragedy in the paper. That's just terrible."

"Well, we're still in business."

"But your building burned down."

"No, not all of it," Derek said. "We've rented some space, and we're carrying on while we rebuild the facility. Thankfully, some of our equipment survived, but the research and development lab and the production area are gone."

"That's a real shame."

"We've entered a new phase, Clyde. I think we all know what Garrett was trying to teach us when he was still here. We've entered a new phase of dedication to our fallen leader, and we're not giving up."

"Well, you carry on, Derek. I'll be waiting to see what happens next. You aren't going to sell the business, are you?"

"Sell?" Derek almost choked on the word. "No, I don't think so."

But Margret had called their meeting today. What did she want to tell them? That she wanted to sell the company? He knew he wasn't the only member of the management team who had mixed feelings about what would happen to Nexus next. It was difficult even thinking about moving the company forward without Garrett.

Derek glanced at his watch. "Clyde, I've gotta go. I've got an important meeting coming up."

After he hung up, he wondered if other members of the management team were having as difficult a time focusing on their jobs as he was. Why had Margret called the meeting? What was she going to present today?

At his desk, he checked his e-mail. Erin had forwarded

a message to the management team. It was the copy of an e-mail Carlton had sent to Margret the day after Garrett's funeral:

Margret,

Please let me first say that I am very sorry for your loss. I have so much remorse for my final interactions with Garrett. I ask for your forgiveness for any undue stress you or Garrett experienced because of my rash actions. I didn't attend the funeral, even though I wanted to. I felt unworthy to take a seat when so many other people deserved to take it. My life has changed in the last week, and I will never be the same. If there's anything I can ever do for you or your family, please let me know.

Thanks,
Carlton

P.S. I never took that job at Health-fuze, Inc. They offered it to me, but I didn't feel right accepting it.

Derek's mind leaped back to that threatening e-mail from Carlton he'd read on Garrett's computer screen shortly before the fire. He wondered if Margret had any idea of the stress Garrett had been carrying during his final days. Maybe he would ask her.

He glanced at his watch. Not long now until the important meeting.

Kramer was also anticipating the morning's meeting when his cell phone rang. The caller ID made him frown in puzzlement. "This is Kramer."

"Kramer, it's Margret Thompson. How are you doing?"

He wasn't sure how best to answer. "I'm fine, I guess—not great—but I'm getting by." Why would she call him an hour before the meeting? She didn't give him long to wonder.

"Kramer, I know about the B228 project."

Tension drained from Kramer's neck, and relief flowed through his veins. He was glad she knew about the project; he'd been unsure of what to do with the product information. "I've got the key information. It was when I went back to save it that I got lost in the smoke."

There was a long pause.

"Kramer, I'm glad you've got that information. If the meeting goes as planned today, I will share information about B228 with the group. But I wanted you to know first. Does anybody else know about it?"

"No, but I think it would encourage the team if you told them."

Margret sighed. "Kramer, I know you still blame yourself a little bit for Garrett's death. I hope you'll let go of that. It wasn't your fault."

He didn't say anything. He waited.

"The B228 project could save many lives," she said. "If you hadn't gone back to get the data, we might never be able to produce this product and help so many people."

Kramer's throat tightened. *Garrett gave his life so many could live.*

He knew he'd struggle with guilty feelings for a while, but Margret's words helped. "Thanks, Margret. I'll see you in an hour."

CHAPTER 16

Unity

Margret entered the conference room to a barrage of warm hugs and well wishes from the Nexus management team. As everyone was seated, Erin opened the meeting. "Margret, I know you called this meeting and that you have an agenda you want to speak to, but we're wondering if we could present something to you first."

Margret searched their somber faces, wondering what they had planned. "Do whatever you like. That's fine."

"Garrett meant a lot to us," Erin said, "and each of us would like to tell you about something he taught us. We each picked one word and want to describe to you how Garrett represented this word to us. Kari, will you go first?"

"Strength," Kari said, misty-eyed. "His strength made all of us strong. He gave us a strength we didn't know we had. He believed in himself and in us. Garrett had a high moral standard because he was strong, not weak. He had strength to hold us to the high standards he had for himself. He was strong enough to be flexible yet strict at the same time. He was always investing in us."

Erin went next. "Humbleness. Garrett's humility was not false humility. He was not a self-serving person who needed to take credit. He always stressed that the team deserved credit. He deflected praise because his self-esteem didn't need the attention. He had pride but not in a personal way. He had pride in us and in what we did together. He thought no job was beneath him. He put himself last."

Next came Derek. Voice husky, eyes wet. "Teamwork. Garrett knew we were stronger together than separate. He strived for us to have unity, even when we didn't always want to conform. His desires and goals steered us. It was hard to be negative when he was continually optimistic. He taught us to build each other up, not to tear others down. Garrett believed hard work was the building block of a great team. He didn't expect anything from us that he didn't expect from himself."

Kramer paused a moment to compose himself. "Authentic. Garrett led with purpose—we knew he believed the mission. He bestowed confidence in us and taught us how to trust. He always pushed us to be lifetime learners and always wanted us to improve. He was fair and had a high moral standard. Garrett always took ownership of his decisions. We followed his leadership because we wanted to, not because he directed us to."

John came last. "Love. Garrett was a servant. He didn't judge others. His desire was to help others, and he taught all of us how to do that. He was patient and kind, and he genuinely cared about all of us, making our team feel like a family. He was always honest and tried to listen before he spoke. He loved us enough to keep us accountable. He was the most generous person we knew. He made me want to be a better man."

Erin stood and crossed to the corner of the room to retrieve a wrapped gift for Margret. As Margret opened it, already deeply moved, her throat tightened. Inside was the professionally printed document the team had just read to her. Matted and framed, it was ready for her to hang on the wall. At the top of the document were the words "Our Inspirational and Influential Leader."

Tears stung her eyes. She'd always known they cared

for Garrett, but the last few weeks had revealed the full impact he'd had on their lives. "Thank you. I'll cherish this always. Now I have something I want to read to you too."

From her navy portfolio, she pulled out a typed document she'd prepared for the team. After clearing her throat and blotting sweaty palms on her skirt, she began reading.

"These weeks since Garrett passed away have felt like a bad dream. It doesn't seem right that he's not still with us. Nonetheless, we need to ask ourselves, 'What would Garrett want?' If he could send us a message, what would it say?" Margret closed her eyes and took a deep breath before resuming. "The Garrett Thompson I knew would want Nexus, Inc., to continue in its mission. He always said we were a team through both good times and bad. I'm sure he would have wanted all of you to take this company to the next level."

She glanced up at them with a smile before continuing. "I have made a couple of decisions in the last week that I want all of you to know about. I decided to take on the responsibility of chair of the board of directors. Garrett would have wanted this. I also called Erin Masden and asked her to assume the position of president of Nexus, Inc. She has graciously accepted."

Margret studied their faces. She'd been anxious about

how the group would respond to her decision. She was pleasantly pleased when everyone cheered, smiled at Erin, and patted her on the back. The approval was unanimous.

Margret continued. "I also want to let you five know that before his death, Garrett planned to set up a stock options program for you. In honor of his wishes, I plan to start that right away." She handed everyone a copy of the new stock plan and sensed their relief and delight at this news.

She cleared her throat. "Finally, I would like to introduce you to the B228 project, something dear to Garrett's heart. I have no idea why Kramer and Garrett called it B228, but I guess that doesn't matter now. What it can possibly do could change the world—and that's no exaggeration. This product, which Nexus plans to develop, will prevent and fight cancer cells."

Collective gasps and astonished faces from everyone but Kramer came as expected. "Yes, that's right. Fight cancer cells." She wet her lips and returned to the document. "The world needs this product, and it's our responsibility to take what Garrett started and continue the mission."

Margret closed the portfolio, then took a deep breath and let it out. She gave them a moment to absorb what she'd shared with them. And absorb they did . . . after a hearty round of applause.

As she searched their faces, she saw what she'd been looking for. Resolve and determination. They understood the new responsibility Garrett would have bestowed on them. They had been through so much in the last few weeks, but it was time to move forward. Strength and unity shone from their earnest faces. It was a clear sign that they were ready to embark on the next phase of the Nexus mission.

Note from the Author: the story behind Nexus

*T*he *Secret of Nexus* is a fictional story loosely based on the life of Jesus Christ and his disciples. The inspiration to write this story came soon after I watched a Passion play with my family during the Easter season. I had always been intrigued by Christ's leadership and tried to implement the styles he modeled into my own leadership. The actor who played Christ that day did a great job showing Christ's leadership to me in a new light.

As business leaders, we often think we have the toughest and most stressful situations to deal with at work. But after watching the Passion play that day, I realized for the first time how tough it must have been to be a leader in Christ's situation. Many people wanted to kill him, and he knew they eventually would. Most people questioned him and were disappointed with the form he came in. One of his closest followers betrayed him. His disciples had many faults. To keep them focused on the task during such a tumultuous time must have been the ultimate task.

I felt led to put what I was feeling on paper. The result is this modern-day story set in a business environment about a leader of an organization who was inspirational and influential. I felt compelled to take the story a step further and allude to some of the same situations Christ experienced with his disciples. I used for the Nexus leadership team many of the same personality traits we find in the twelve disciples. What I discovered is that many of the disciples had trust issues; that's why you see those issues appear in the book more than other negative characteristics.

You can see a parallel between Carlton and Judas. Just as Judas betrayed Jesus, Carlton betrayed Garrett in the Nexus. Most of the Nexus team struggled with life issues, just as the real disciples did—just as we all do. Holding employees accountable is not always easy, but we do them a disfavor by overlooking situations that need to be addressed. Though Christ's teachings were not always comfortable to hear, the people needed them.

Nexus, Inc. was developing a product to cure cancer and possibly save countless lives. That cure is a metaphor of our faith. Jesus came to earth to give the greatest gift to anyone who wanted it, rich or poor. Garrett's goal was a cure for cancer, and he wanted to make it available for everyone, not just for those who were rich. Obviously, we don't have a cure-all for every form of cancer in this world; this was only my analogy. In the story, Garrett was fairly certain that the medical field would reject their cure for cancer because it was not in the form the world would expect it to come in. This is also how many people viewed Jesus Christ and why many rejected him.

Jesus prepared his disciples for their earthly mission. Garrett prepared his team, the Nexus 6, so they could take a life-saving product to the needy masses.

Garrett's father, Tom Cooper, made the decision to give up his only son because he loved him so much and wanted him to have a better life. Our Father in heaven also gave his only Son, Jesus, so that we may be saved from our sins and enjoy life everlasting. Jesus sacrificed his own life for ours by dying on the cross. In this story, saving an employee and the cure for cancer from the fire cost Garrett Thompson his life. Garrett's life and death represent the Christian's purpose of living for the Lord.

The hidden truth of leadership is we need to follow the example of Christ, and lead as Jesus led his disciples here on this earth.

Inspirational and Influential Leadership

How can we influence those we work with—not because of the position we hold but by the way we lead? How do we encourage people to follow us—because we inspire them to and not because they have to?

There are many types of leadership styles: authoritative, charismatic, hands-on, and servant leadership are just a few. Although each of us is probably dominated by one leadership style, good leaders should possess a little of each style because all are needed at different times. Jesus Christ would probably be considered a servant leader, but at times he exhibited other styles as well.

The individuals we manage are different and unique, and they respond differently to different styles of leadership. As described in chapter 3, a good leader has the ability to manage individuals differently, and this flexibility requires us to use multiple leadership styles to be truly influential.

Influential leadership is the power to give guidance and direction in a way that produces positive actions and behavior in others.

Leadership involves power. How did Garrett Thompson demonstrate power? His power came from many things: being humble, sacrificing for others, being a good listener, and investing in his staff. These building blocks led to other attributes such as being knowledgeable, loving people enough to keep them accountable, believing in oneself, building up other people's confidence, fostering teamwork, and being optimistic.

Garrett Thompson's leadership team described him as authentic. People want to be led by someone who is genuine. We have the opportunity to influence others in a positive way every day. Don't waste that opportunity.

Acknowledgements

I would like to take this opportunity to thank my family.

Through my entire life my parents have been incredibly supportive. Growing up in their home gave me a firm foundation in Jesus Christ, the most valuable gift anyone has ever given me. I would like to thank them for their advice and input during the writing of this book.

I have the opportunity to work every day with my brothers Lance and Joel & my brother-in-law Randi Yoder in our family business. I appreciate them reading through the original manuscripts and giving me valuable input. My two sisters, Sharman & Anita, and my sister-in-law Krista Coulter have all also lent me a lot of support and advice during this project. I love you all very much.

Chapter Reflection Questions

CHAPTER 1:
What is your company culture like?

CHAPTER 2:
In what ways is your team diverse?

CHAPTER 3:
How are you keeping your employees accountable?

CHAPTER 4:
Which jobs do you consider to be beneath you?

CHAPTER 5:
How are you rewarding your employees?

CHAPTER 14:

In what ways do your actions show that you truly care for others?

CHAPTER 15:

Is your message being heard?

CHAPTER 16:

How would your staff describe you?

For more information about
Jeff J. Miller
&

The Secret of Nexus
please visit:

www.JeffJMiller.com
Jeff@thesecretofnexus.com
www.facebook.com/TheSecretOfNexus
@JeffJayMiller